SIX PLAYS

BY MAVOR MOORE

"A Canadian cultural giant" — ABE

Talonbooks　　•　　Vancouver　　•　　1989

Published with assistance from the Canada Council

Talonbooks
201/1019 East Cordova
Vancouver
British Columbia V6A 1M8
Canada

Typeset in Baskerville by Pièce de Résistance Ltée. Printed and bound in Canada by Hignell Printing Ltd.

First printing October 1989.

Canadian Cataloguing in Publication Data

Moore, J. Mavor, 1919-
   Six Plays by Mavor Moore

   ISBN 0-88922-271-1

   I. Title.   II. Title: Six plays by Mavor Moore.
PS8526.063S5 1989   C812'.54   C89-091574-1
PR9199.3.M63S5 1989

CONTENTS

INTRODUCTION

This collection of plays for two actors is more than another attempt to meet the pressing demand for theatrical economy. The six plays are linked by a common concern with the interplay of three different perspectives on reality: what is being said, what appears to be happening, and what the audience is doing.

"The Apology," which I wrote before I. F. Stone's *The Trial of Socrates* revived interest in this first legal test of freedom of expression, was forever cast in the form of a two-hander by Plato, from whom I stole it. Plato's *The Apology*, an eyewitness account of Socrates' self-defense, has always been considered a literary masterpiece — perhaps because it has most often been translated by scholars determined to turn the blunt stonemason into a scholiast. But Plato, like Pope John Paul II, was a dramatist before he attained the rank of philospher. And ever since I first encountered Plato's dialogues in old Greek, as a student, I've perceived the structure of *The Apology*, especially, as that of a drama.

It consists, after all, of a situation that develops step by step as the result of an interplay between the main character, his predicament and his judges. As the trial progresses, Socrates moves from jaunty confidence to anger to ironic serenity in response to the shifting ground of the argument and the changing mood of his hearers. Although given no lines by Plato, his fellow citizens, as hecklers, supporters and judges, are essential elements in the action.

The confrontation, moreover, pits the individual against the collective — a subject of keen interest in our own day. How tolerant of gadflies can democracies afford to be? Put another way, how much impertinence will an audience take before it explodes or dissolves? This is a question one cannot answer in the library. There's no need to modernize the setting to discover the immediacy of this drama, or to find it at home in the theatre's eternal present.

My "Apology" is a recent work, not yet performed except as a reading — mainly because I've wanted to try it out, in some detail, on and with various audiences. The five shorter pieces in this volume were all written at an earlier period: between 1968 and 1974. But they share a similar focus on the no man's land between dialogue, dramatic action and "the house." They are explorations of the fascinating three-part counterpoint between the figure, the ground, and the observer sitting in another time-space frame.

In the 1950's and 1960's I had been busier helping to launch a television network and various theatrical enterprises than I had been writing plays for them to present. What playwriting I did leaned toward the spectacular and the musical, culminating in 1967, Canada's centennial year, in the "Louis Riel" that composer Harry Somers and I wrote for the Canadian Opera Company. After that monumental libretto I felt the need to work on a smaller scale. I had in mind, for my sins, a series of short plays on the seven types of ambiguity.

True to the times in Canada, I wrote versions of each for radio, television and theatre, hoping to sell the plays to one and then the others in order of luck. This strategy had the additional advantage. I kept telling myself, of allowing me to examine the esthetic differences between these arts. The theatre, my fondest target, was naturally the least likely to return the investment in time and paper. So while all of them were conceived for the theatre, "The Argument," "Getting In," "The Store" (which has two extra minor characters) and "Come Away, Come Away" made their debuts on both electronic media before appearing as stageplays. "The Pile," written as a stageplay (with the live audience analogized in its title), was first heard on radio, and has never — the joke simply wouldn't work — been seen on television.

Thanks to that remarkable London literary agent, the late Jimmy Wax, mentor of Christopher Fry, Harold Pinter and other princes of the realm, these plays found acceptance abroad and have received a number of productions in other languages. "Getting In," the stage version of which first appeared in the United States, seems to flag a particularly universal angst; it was recently produced in Urdu.

It is the stage versions of the plays that are collected, for the first time, in this Talonbooks anthology. But I must thank such former CBC provocateurs as Robert Weaver, radio director Jean Bartels and television producer Fletcher Markle, as well as Martin Esslin and Anne Head of the BBC, for giving the plays their first performances.

May "The Apology" have its premiere in the theatre, where it belongs.

Mavor Moore
Vancouver, 1989

THE APOLOGY

a play in Two Acts

based on the reports by Plato and Xenophon
of Socrates' defence at his trial in Athens, 399 B.C.

Persons in the play:
Socrates
Meletus

The Apology has been given three readings by the author:

- in 1987 in Victoria, B.C., at Open Space, with David Veniot as Meletus;

- in 1988 in London, England, at Canada House, with Garrick Hagon as Meletus;

- in 1989 in Vancouver, B.C., at The New Play Centre, with Mitch Mulloy as Meletus.

ACT ONE

A platform in Athens, 399 B.C. — vacant, when we see it in the light, except for a stunted pillar in the centre, which performs the function of a leaning-post for the speaker and possibly a repository for notes. Seated in the FAR RIGHT of the audience, isolated, are four JUDGES. On its LEFT, at the other side, are Socrates' three accusers: ANYTUS, LYCON and MELETUS. The youngest of them, the poet Meletus, rises and mounts the platform. He turns to face the assembly, first bowing to the Judges facing him.

MELETUS:

Honourable Judges, fellow citizens of Athens. This trial need never have taken place. We've been very reluctant to bring this action against such a popular man. Anytus, Lycon and I have taken the initiative because no one in these testing times should be allowed to undermine public confidence in democratic government and get away with it. You've heard my colleagues. I'll simply sum up the charges.

In a sentence, Socrates has broken the law, mocked the gods, and corrupted young people with false teaching. Legally, this is a classic case of fraud: a man doing harm to others while he pretends to be doing good. In the name of good government he promotes sedition, in the name of religion he preaches blasphemy, and in the name of education he tells lies.

Now let me say at once that this isn't a question of personal animosity: Anytus is a politician, Lycon's a teacher, and I'm a poet — so we cover a wide spectrum of public opinion. We believe Socrates has abused the right of every Athenian to free speech, because he uses it to blacken the Athens that guarantees that right.

The point is: how far can tolerance go in democracy? Is society an apple that has to put up with a worm at its core; nibbling away, saying it's nonsense to elect governors and judges by counting ballots? According to Socrates, if you believe in choosing leaders by popularity contests instead of merit, you should choose pilots or architects or doctors by ballot — because their mistakes aren't as serious as mistakes made by governments. Now that's a funny line, but he's not joking.

And his cynical ideas have incited younger men to violence. Critias and Alcibiades, the two most arrogant and irresponsible leaders we ever had, were both pupils of Socrates. That's the destructive power of this man's eloquence. It's contagious. With respect, I beg you not to be taken in by it as he addresses you now.   *He bows to the Judges, leaves the stage, and resumes his seat with his fellow accusers.*

> *SOCRATES enters, wary but not intimidated, since he has many supporters in the house. He is seventy years old. His customary shabby clothes and bare feet show little respect for formality. This odd appearance, and his amiable smiling as he takes centre stage and looks about him, elicit some amusement, He nods to friends in the audience. He has no prepared speech or written notes of any kind; but sometimes rests on the short pillar. He is respectful to the Judges, but looks at his accusers only when making a point at their expense. Conscious of the incongruity of the scene, he bows and hesitates.*

SOCRATES:
How . . . er — How you . . . er . . .   *He shakes his head in amusement.*   How you people of Athens feel about that speech and the others, about these accusations, I have no idea, I um . . . I um . . .   *He chuckles.*   They're so plausible! — almost made me forget who I am. But you know, there isn't a word of truth in it. So many lies have been told, I scarcely know where to start. Umm. I suppose the oddest is telling you to be on your guard against my eloquence. Ha! To say a thing like that, when they'd be found out the moment I open my mouth. That takes courage. And brass. Unless, of course, what they mean by 'the power of eloquence' is 'the power of truth' — in which case they're absolutely right: I am eloquent.

Because what you'll get from me is the truth — and it won't be all decked out in legal jargon. It'll be the plain truth in my own plain words, and not a piece cobbled together by some speechwriter. *A look at Meletus.*

You think that's unfair? At my age, let me tell you, fellow citizens, it would make no sense for me to present myself as an acrobat. I was never what you'd call a smooth orator. Never learned the tricks. This old dog is over seventy, and in court for the first time in his life — at least on this side of the fence. I can only bark the way I always have. So you'll just have to forgive my homespun manners, the way you'd excuse a traveller in your house. If anyone here finds that awkward, possibly even impertinent, I'd ask him to concentrate on what I'm saying and not on how. Is that all right? I hope we can all agree on that. *Cheerfully:* My life is the one at stake!

Let me reply, first, to the old charges. Very old, most of them — naturally, because over the years I've collected critics the way most people collect flowers. I've collected a lot of thorns! *Laughs.* The new ones — men like Anytus: ah, there you are! — the new crop is bad enough, but not as dangerous as the old burrs that latched onto you when you were still boys, and addled your minds with gossip about a lunatic called Socrates — *to head off objections:* — I said 'called' Socrates! Not the real one but a mythical monster, a fantasy, a rumour, who was supposed to go around spouting blasphemy — all sorts of peculiar theories about who's in heaven and what's inside the earth — and generally putting up good cases for bad causes. So it's these accusers, these old accusers, if you know who I mean, who are really dangerous — partly because they lump together all those who don't conform, for whatever reason, and call them 'atheists,' and partly because . . . Well, I've no wish to lump *them* together, but I've no alternative, because the law won't allow me to name names. *Pause.* Not even in the case of a well-known writer of comedies, who shall be nameless. Unless you happen to know it.

Outraged. I am not allowed! I am not allowed to get them up here and cross-examine them; I have to box with shadows, with ghosts out of the past. And so my case goes by default, as it always has, and I'm left attempting to clear away in a hour the accumulated slander of a lifetime. Not easy. Not easy.

From dark reverie, he suddenly spins on his audience.   I heard that! I heard you say 'Aristophanes' — I wasn't going to mention the name, but of course you're right. I'm sorry it slipped out, but there it is. In that play of his *The Clouds*, the playwright 'A' introduces a character he calls Socrates. You remember? Now . . . this idiot called Socrates spends all his waking hours in a basket . . . sitting in a big portable basket . . . sometimes suspended in the air . . . spewing out to anyone who'll listen a stream of double-talk about everything under the sun — totally beyond your ken and mine. He does! — in the play, that is. Now I have no quarrel with students of the physical sciences — it's simply that I never touch them. How could I? — I'm not a scientist of any kind, let alone a sham one. Anyone who has ever heard me speak will vouch for my sheer, unadultered ignorance of science. And most of the other tall tales spun by playwright 'A' come out of the same bottle. Very funny stuff, but the truth gets a little . . . bubbly.   *He laughs ruefully.*

Like the story that I'm a professional teacher. As Lycon is. I have nothing whatever against teachers. I greatly admire many of them — good heavens!   *A warm gesture to Lycon.*   If someone really knows enough about life to educate others, and can collect a fee for doing it, I say more power to him. If I could do it, I would. But as it is, I've nothing to sell — at any rate, no information of the sort most people are prepared to pay for.   *He looks around benignly.*   Would you? You? Well, there you are.

Now some of you may be saying — I don't mean to misinterpret those little noises — but some of you may be saying, in effect, 'That's all very well, Socrates, but where there's smoke there's fire, and for all those nasty rumours to start you must have done something peculiar.' Or you may be thinking, 'We don't want to judge you hastily, old fellow, but you can hardly stand up there with a straight face and tell us you're an ordinary man, like a million others, nothing unusual about you at all. If you won't tell people what you're up to, how can you blame them for drawing their own conclusions?' That sort of thing. Well,

12

I think that's a fair challenge. I think it *is* up to me to explain why some people call me a wise man, some call me a wiseacre, and others call me a halfwit. I mean — look at me!   *Then, taking exception to the laughter:*   I know I'm plain. Like the truth. And you will get the truth from me, as I promised. The truth is that . . . in a way, in one particular but important sense . . . I *am* wise. Now go ahead. Those so inclined have half a minute to jeer.   *He waits.*   Thank you.

The secret is quite simple: I am as wise as a man can be.   *He lets this sink in.*   If you follow me. Not wise in the superhuman sense, like some of your statesmen and academics . . . I hope I'm not offending anybody, and if I am you have every right to object, because I have no idea what I'm talking about. I have never, in all my life, run across superhuman wisdom. Not in a human being, at any rate. I think I'd be disappointed in superhuman wisdom if I did. But there's no getting around the fact — at least everybody tells me it's a fact — that I have some reputation for human-scale wisdom . . . the sort of wisdom that's within our reach if only we can bring ourselves to realize it. Would you like my explanation? Would you?   *He encourages a response.*   Then bear with me while I introduce a witness whose word is beyond question: Apollo, the God who speaks to us at his shrine in Delphi. Here is the story.   *A pause.*

You all knew Chaerophon — you must have. Chaerophon was one of my oldest friends, a friend of democracy, a friend of Athens, a friend in good times and bad. But, you know, he was an impetuous sort of man; he'd get an idea and —   *Snap.*   — off he'd go after it. Remember? Well one day Chaerophon took it into his head to go to Delphi and put a question to the Oracle. Nothing odd about that . . . nothing odd except the question he wanted to put. The question he asked the resident priestess was . . . whether there was any man wiser than Socrates. I'm quite aware it sounds absurd — but it was Chaerophon's idea, not mine. So no one can blame me for the Oracle's reply. She is supposed to be speaking for the God; and when he asked her whether there was any man wiser than Socrates, she said 'No, there is not.' Now . . . !

13

He addresses himself, in mime, to one part of the assembly after another, shrugging, raising his eyes aloft, spreading his hands in innocence, laughing at the absurdity of it all, implicitly asking how he could be blamed, declaring his detachment from any such idea, eventually smiling ruefully at his inability to convince all present.

Chaerophon's dead, of course. But if you doubt me, ask his brother — he's here today — he'll tell you the story is absolutely true. *Pause.* But I know how you feel. It's exactly how *I* felt when I heard about it later. 'What can the God mean?' I asked myself: 'What is he hinting at?' Gods only speak in riddles, of course, and I realized I had to winkle out the meaning of this particular riddle. But where to begin? I knew I had no *real* wisdom, give or take a few grains of common sense; so how could I possibly be the wisest man alive? On the other hand, it was impossible for me to believe the God was lying. Gods never lie. Gods never *need* to lie, because the truth is exactly what they decide to make it. All right, I said to myself: 'Then it must be an honest mistake.' Well — ! Come now! *He holds his head as his laughter explodes.* What an idea! I mean, how do you approach the Almighty, respectfully, on your knees, bowing your head, holding out a sacrificial bowl, and say: 'Terribly sorry, Majesty, but haven't you made a ghastly mistake?' *Dissolves in laughter again as he acts it out, but pulls himself together.* No disrespect . . . no disrespect intended, fellow citizens. I'm laughing at myself, not at the gods. *Having been forced into the humiliation of explaining his joke, he goes soberly and intensely to the point.*

It was then that I struck on a way of handling it — a diplomatic way, I thought, that might save face for all concerned, 'If only I can find a man wiser than myself,' I concluded, 'I could go back to the God with something in my hand like a solid reason for doubt, and ask him humbly but straightforwardly to explain what he meant. So when I —

MELETUS: *from where he is: sitting.*
That's blasphemy!

SOCRATES:
Call it blasphemy if you like, my friend — but remember the

14

God's words! The God has spoken, and it was up to me, with all the honesty and piety I could muster, to find out what he had in mind! *Angrily, he looks about for other challengers. There are none. Meletus subsides.*

Thank you. I will tell you now what I did. *Realizing they expect him to be utterly serious, he cannot resist the temptation to throw more straight-faced darts.* I started, so to speak, at the top. *Looking directly at Anytus:* With a politician. *Getting his laugh, he attacks the laughers.* No, no — I mean I picked a politician with a reputation. — No, not *that* kind of reputation: I mean a reputation for political wisdom — and I went to have a talk with him. You know, a politician who is really good at his job is a beautiful thing. I have the highest admiration for all things that fulfill their proper function. So I gave him the benefit of the doubt. But after a few minutes' conversation I realized that was a mistake. He wasn't wise at all, although obviously a good many people thought he was, including himself. *As his sallies win some response, he begins to enjoy the game immensely, joining in the laughter at his own jokes.* I tried to explain to him — gently, because he was a decent man — I tried to show him he wasn't as wise as he thought, but he couldn't understand why I'd come unless I wanted a favour, and this seemed to him a peculiar way of asking. When he realized I hadn't come to pat him on the back he was furious, and had his servant show me out the back door. I'd made an enemy for life! — quite a few, actually, because a lot of people had voted for him believing he was as wise as he claimed he was, and didn't want to admit they'd made a mistake. *Laughing.* Oh, they hated me!

On the way home I said to myself, 'I don't suppose either of us knows anything worth much — but I may be a notch better off than he is. He thinks he knows something and doesn't, while I know nothing and can't even be sure of that.' Then I thought, perhaps I just hit on a poor sort of a leader, struck the runt of the litter. So I went across to the home of a rich man, a merchant, a man of commerce who owns a whole fleet of trading ships and a hundred slaves — a solid citizen who knows the real world, understands what makes people clink. Well, we talked, and we talked . . . and I'm obliged to tell you I eventually came to the same conclusion about my captain of commerce: he was an ignoramus about everything except money, and what and whom it could buy. So I made another lifetime enemy there, and all of *his* friends into the bargain. Did you ever notice that powerful men have a great many friends? *Cockily, he studies the assembly for a long moment, glancing intermittently at his accusers.*

Understand me, please: I had no thought of going around the city making enemies. It wasn't my idea: the God had given me a mission. I can't help it if the mission made me enemies. Actually, my mission so far was extremely discouraging — depressing, even. I'd found that the men with the highest reputation were usually those with the lowest intelligence, and vice versa. I'm trying to show you, you see, that I was on a genuine quest, like the labours of Hercules, to find out if the Oracle's riddle made any sense. And I'm not singling out those in public life — because after I'd talked to the politicians and the merchants I tackled the poets. *And he sweeps Meletus with a wicked smile.*

> *MELETUS, in his front row seat, mumbles something savage to his colleagues. Aware that he is likely to be used as a stooge by a master dialectician, he has been bracing himself for the ordeal. He is cautious, cool, and very much on guard. SOCRATES becomes elaborately naive.*

SOCRATES:
'Now here,' I said to myself, 'you'll be found out in no time. There is absolutely no doubt that you're more in the dark than the poets.' I mean, they can see things . . . they can see things the rest of us scarcely glimpse. Deep things — like authentic suffering, and ultimate truth. And they find such marvellous ways of expressing what they've seen, as anyone can tell from reading those brilliant verses and romances and tragedies, full of . . . insight! . . . and understanding! *Pause.* So before I went I looked up a few well-turned passages, a few of those daisy-chains of profundities they're so good at, and took them with me. And I asked the various authors what they meant. *His eyes grow wide with amazement.*

16

MELETUS:
Answer the charges!

SOCRATES:
No, honestly, I hoped they could teach me. I did. And I take no pleasure in telling you today — I'm embarrassed to have to say it — but anyone here could have shed more light on those poems than their authors did. *He suddenly laughs at the thought.* It's true! Oh, I knew, of course, that poets don't write with their brains. They're not really in conscious control when those words come out of their mouths. They work — and they say this themselves — they work as a sort of human conduit for divine inspiration. They're like soothsayers or prophets, who hand you a bunch of keys with no notion themselves of what doors they're likely to fit. And that is, genuinely, a great contribution to society: the keys open all kinds of doors you didn't even know were there! *Pause.* But these poets, you see — these poets told me they did use their brains. Three or four of them said their brains were 'prodigious' — that was the word they used — and all their readers had told them so. Their readers told them they were prodigious, and they believed them. They knew not only all about writing poetry, but all about the subjects they wrote poems about — all about everything, in a word. And they not only knew all about everything, they understood it, perfectly! The only thing they didn't understand, so far as I could see, was themselves. And so I left them, deeply depressed, and with a new crop of enemies. Not only the poets, naturally; none of their readers cared to admit they'd been taken in, either.

MELETUS:
Honourable Judges, if this man —

SOCRATES:
You're quite right, Meletus. *To the Judges:* Here's the point. My quest was failing. I still had no idea of what the God was getting at. None. And until I had, there was no rest for me. So I went to visit some artists — craftsmen, artisans, honest tradesmen who work with their hands. I'll tell you: I have a natural affection for artistic skill; I'm a stonemason, as some of you know. But I know all too little about my own art, and

nothing whatever about others. I've no notion of weaving and painting and metal work and singing and all that. How they put this and that together and achieve the effects they do, is beyond me. I'm envious; I respect their talents. And I discovered I was right, when I talked to them. They knew all sorts of things I didn't know. They were much wiser than I could possibly be in everything connected with their own line of work.

But . . . how else can I put it? . . . the more I questioned them, the more they became like the politicians and merchants and poets. Just because they were authorities on painting a picture or playing the harp, they got it into their heads they were authorities on politics and commerce, on war and science and religion. They had opinions on every subject — and the weaker the grasp, the stronger the opinion. The slowest of the lot could tell the government how to govern, the generals how to win wars, the astronomers how to count stars and the priests how to pray. *Sincerely.* I really am sorry if I'm offending any of my fellow artists — but you know, honestly, as a rule artists are impossibly self-centred! *Aside to the Judges:* Irrelevant: I know. *Up:* Well, my friends, I retreated from the artists — I ran away, I fled, having made several more lifetime enemies. Including all those who make a living talking and writing about art, as if it were the envelope in which life is a mere letter. *To an intake of breath from a critic in the house:* I'm sorry if I . . .

As I ran — and I was literally running down the streets — I remember asking myself whether I really wanted to go on with this. Here I was, caught like a wretched fly between knowing too much and too little about the bottle he's in. Couldn't I just, for example, pretend that I *am* wise, as other people do? But I heard the words of the Oracle in my ear and knew I could never pretend. The only reason people call me wise is that when they talk to me they begin to realize they know less than they thought, and they imagine I've collected what they're missing. If they stopped to think, they'd realize that only a god can do that. And the God, in his wisdom, presented me with this riddle to show us all that human wisdom is worth very little.

MELETUS: *Rising swiftly.*
Including the Honourable Judges'?   *As SOCRATES starts
to answer, then pauses:*   Are you wiser than they are, Socrates?

SOCRATES: *Quietly.*
The God wasn't talking about me — he was just using my name
by way of illustration; making the point, if you like, that the only
wise human being is one who recognizes, as Socrates does, that
his so-called wisdom is trivial. That's all.

MELETUS:
Trivial.   *Glancing at the Judges, he sits down again, satisfied.*

SOCRATES: *Filled suddenly with a towering rage.*
You have called my life into question. You have charged me with
mocking the gods, and with corrupting men.   *To all:*
I am telling you what I do! In obedience to divine command,
not following my own ends, I travel in search of true wisdom.
I make enquiries here. I track a scent there. I ask young and
old, citizen and stranger, what makes them wise. I ask them what
makes others *think* they're wise. When I find that so-and-so is
not wise after all, then, in obedience to the divine command,
I must - show - him - up!   *Then, as suddenly ashamed of his out-
burst — he has handed Meletus a second point — he takes a moment to
calm himself and recapture his more comfortable ground of self-mockery.*

Well. My full-time occupation, you might say, is making
enemies. I'm an upsetter of apple-carts, a general nuisance. But
whatever you happen to think of it, my occupation occupies me
night and day — which is more than some people can say. It
leaves me no time for public affairs, no time for my family. Ask
my wife. We owe our poverty to divine will, I keep telling her.
I think she half believes me. Every day I'm out plying people
with questions — and this is where the fables start about my
playing wolf to the local lambs.

I'm poor, but I attract rich students: bored sons of well-to-do
families, who find some kind of thrill in my tough question-and-
answer sessions — which I gather no one subjects them to at
home. They work up an imitation of my method, and go around
trying it out on others. They find plenty of easy marks, naturally,

because there are plenty of know-it-alls who know nothing. But once they're exposed, these easy marks never blame the clown who tricked them: they blame me! 'This terrible Socrates,' they cry, 'this charlatan, this public enemy, this ravager of youth!' But if anyone asks 'What sort of thing does he actually do?,' they can point to nothing juicier than the old lies about looney philosophers — every one of them a knucklehead, spinning wild theories about the cosmos when they can't recall the time of day, splitting hairs with no more conscience than a farmer's wife plucking a goose, and daring the gods to strike them dead if they don't like it. And then they tack these hoary old slanders onto me — all because they can't face the poverty of their own intelligence. *He pauses: is he getting the point across?* And what did I do to merit all this attention? Why, I found them out! I found them out! But there's a whole army of these masterminds — ambitious, well placed, well organized, highly vocal . . . *He senses the wall of resistence out there, begins to shout.* . . . and over the years they've stuffed your ears with so much dung that my voice can not get through to you! . . .

He has overdone it, shown his vulnerability to friends and enemies alike; he turns away from the assembly, takes a moment to pull himself together. It is his first premonition of self-inflicted defeat. He shakes it off, but the initial merriment is gone. MELETUS is relaxing.

SOCRATES:

Let's have done with the old accusations, the dirt worked into the corners of the mind, and get on with the new drivel. *Businesslike:* Meletus says there is 'no personal animosity' here. I wonder. You haven't mentioned your son, Anytus. *To the assembly:* A troubled boy — used to follow me about, trying to pick up hints of how to think straight. Not easy, when your father's a politician . . . and your mother's given up. Anytus blames me instead of himself that the boy ran away. Lycon, of course — well, every teacher of public speaking in the city is in a dreadful huff because I've exposed all their trade secrets. And Meletus is a poet. *Shrugs doubtfully.* Now together these three disinterested parties have sworn something to the effect that Socrates is an evil genius who goes around leading impressionable youngsters astray, scoffing at the national religion and promoting some newfangled deities of his own invention. Oh yes, and he wants to destroy the city he lives in. I'm paraphrasing a bit but that's the gist of the charge . . . brought against me, as I've said, by these three totally unprejudiced observers.

But you've got the wrong man. Meletus used the word 'fraud' to describe me . . . and that's interesting because 'fraud' is a word I'd use, in the present circumstances, to describe Meletus . . .

MELETUS: *Rising.*
Fraud?

SOCRATES:
. . . who's pretending right now to care very deeply about something he doesn't care a fig about — and sanctimoniously drags people into court over matters he's shown no interest in before.

MELETUS: *Well pinked.*
That is a lie!

SOCRATES:
Then we'd better find out, Meletus, hadn't we!   *He has succeeded in dragging Meletus into a dialogue.*   The law says I may question you. Are you ready for that?

MELETUS:
Anytime. You can't intimidate me.

SOCRATES:
I can understand that.

MELETUS: *Joining Socrates on stage.*
I doubt it.

SOCRATES:
Good. Now.   *The master:*   Do I take it from what you say, Meletus, that you *do* give some thought to young people and their needs?

21

MELETUS:
Yes. I do.

SOCRATES:
How to develop their potential, improve themselves?

MELETUS:
What else would I be doing?

SOCRATES:
I've no idea. And are you the only one thinking about all that?

MELETUS:
Of course not.

SOCRATES:
Then I wish you'd give us a list of the others, because these Honourable Judges are going to no end of trouble to learn whether I'm on it or not. I'm the worm in the apple: right? Perhaps we could find who's the worm by a process of elimination.   *No response.*   Has the cat got your tongue, Meletus? You said you were deeply concerned about all this, I thought.

MELETUS: *Hotly.*
I am.

SOCRATES:
Then speak up.

MELETUS:
It's not . . . It's not a . . . It's not something . . .

SOCRATES:
Then what is it? Who are all these improvers? Then name one.

MELETUS:
The laws.

SOCRATES:
Oh, good. *Very* good. And who is it who applies these laws?

MELETUS:

The judges, Socrates.

SOCRATES:

You mean the Judges here today? These Honourable gentlemen?

MELETUS:

Yes, among others.

SOCRATES:

All of them — they're all good influences on the young?

MELETUS:

All the judges: yes.

SOCRATES:

Oh, that's good news. We've plenty of improvers, then. Now what about Senators?

MELETUS:

What about them?

SOCRATES:

Do they improve the character of the young?

MELETUS:

The Senators? — of course they do.

SOCRATES:

All of them? I mean, aren't there one or two . . .

MELETUS:

Is that an innuendo? If you have specific charges to lay . . .

SOCRATES:

Oh no . . . no! I'm sure every last Senator is beyond reproach. And of course, the members of the Assembly?

MELETUS:

Yes, they set a good example.

SOCRATES:

And all the citizens here today: I suppose they're improvers too?

MELETUS:

Right.

SOCRATES:

Marvellous.

MELETUS:

Yes, it is. This is leading nowhere.

SOCRATES:

So just about every citizen of Athens, you'd say, is busy improving and uplifting and purifying the youth of Athens, except me. I'm the only polluter in town. Is that your thesis?

MELETUS:

You're by far the worst.

SOCRATES:

That's not what you said. Are you prepared to name others?

MELETUS:

You're the one on trial here.

SOCRATES:

So I am. Thank you for making that so clear. Then what about horses?

MELETUS:

Horses?

SOCRATES:

Is one person a bad influence on horses, and nobody else?

MELETUS:

What in hell do horses have to do with it?

SOCRATES:

Is it the same with them? Is one man ruining all the colts and fillies, while everyone else is busy improving the stock?

MELETUS:
  With horses, not exactly.

SOCRATES:
  What do you mean by 'not exactly'? Isn't it the other way round?

MELETUS:
  What do you mean by 'the other way round'?

SOCRATES:
  That only one person is likely to do them any good — a horse trainer. People with no experience of horses are more likely to do them harm.

MELETUS:
  You don't need to be a chicken to raise eggs.

SOCRATES:
  Maybe, but you'd better know something about chicks. Now. What youth work have you been engaged in lately?

MELETUS:
  That's irrelevant.

SOCRATES:
  I was just thinking how glorious it'd be for young Athenians if they had only one bad influence — a lone worm, one single cancer in a body politic shining with spiritual muscle. But I don't think you know anything about young Athenians.
  As MELETUS starts to reply: Next question. Meletus: is it better to live in a good community or a bad one?

MELETUS:
  Will you stay with the subject?

SOCRATES:
  Oh come on: that's an easy one.   *To a child.*   Let me put it another way. Don't good neighbours help each other, and bad neighbours . . .

MELETUS: *Interrupting.*

It's a stupid question!

SOCRATES:

Never mind: the law says you must answer to the best of your ability. *Looks heavenward at the prospect.* Let's try again. Do you know anyone who likes being harmed by his neighbours?

MELETUS:

No, I don't.

SOCRATES:

Then let me ask you: When you accuse me of corrupting the innocent, are you saying I do it deliberately?

MELETUS:

Yes.

SOCRATES:

You sure?

MELETUS:

I'm sure.

SOCRATES:

But I thought you just said that —

MELETUS:

Don't put words in my mouth!

SOCRATES:

Do you take them back?

MELETUS:

Take what back?

SOCRATES:

The words: that good neighbours help each other and bad ones —

MELETUS: *Curtly.*
    No, I stand by that.

SOCRATES:
    Good. *Very* good. Not easy to grasp, that point.

MELETUS: *Becoming frantically wary.*
    What point?

SOCRATES:
    That if I succeeded in harming my neighbour, he'd become a
    bad neighbour and do *me* harm. Yet you say I'd do that
    deliberately.

MELETUS: *After grim reflection.*
    What I said was . . . What I said . . .

SOCRATES: *Sympathetically.*
    Hard to remember, isn't it.

MELETUS: *Blowing up.*
    It was you who said it! Either you harm them, or —

SOCRATES: *Interrupting: hard.*
    — Either I do not harm them, Meletus, or I do it unintentionally.
    Now you know as well as I that this High Court never deals with
    unintentional offences: intention has to be proved. Have you
    proved it, you and your friends?

MELETUS:
    We don't have to prove the obvious. You were going around
    leading innocent young people astray —

SOCRATES:
    To your own knowledge?

MELETUS:
    I've seen you at it, yes — with your . . . parasites.

SOCRATES:
    Did you ever report it?

MELETUS:

Why should I!

SOCRATES:

As a concerned citizen. Either that, or you should have taken me aside, quietly, and told me that if I didn't mend my ways you'd be forced to turn me in. Perhaps if I'd had good advice like that I would have quit doing whatever I was doing unintentionally in the first place. But you didn't open your mouth — either to me or to the authorities, I think you said. Call yourself a concerned citizen — where was your concern then? It didn't exist until you hale me into court, where they hand out sentences instead of neighbourly advice.

MELETUS:

Do you honestly believe nobody commits a crime intentionally? Using that excuse a complete monster could say he didn't know any better. I think you do know better.

SOCRATES:

As I've said, I know nothing.   *Then hard:*   But you say you do! And I want some specifics from you — some details of how I'm supposed to have corrupted an entire generation by teaching people to sneer at religion and the gods. Have I got it right? I'm supposed to be a blasphemer and an atheist, am I, according to you three?

MELETUS:

The wording in the indictment is perfectly clear.

SOCRATES: *Mock-innocent.*

Oh. Perfectly clear. Then perhaps I'm being . . . Perhaps you could clarify one point for me, then, and for the Honourable Judges. I'm not sure whether you mean that I teach my flock to worship *no* gods, which *would* make me both a blasphemer and an atheist; or to abondon your gods in favour of some others, in which case I might be accused of blasphemy but certainly not of atheism; or to worship any gods you like, so long as you live a virtuous life — in which case I couldn't possibly be either a blasphemer or an atheist. I'm confused about that.

MELETUS: *Smiling.*
I'm not surprised. A man who hears voices in his head . . . *He addresses the Assembly.* He goes around saying the sun is made of stone and the moon's made of earth!

SOCRATES:
There we go again! Same old story. You're mixing me up with someone else, Meletus — probably Anaxagoras.

MELETUS:
Never read him.

SOCRATES:
Yes, but the Judges may have. Not everyone's as illiterate as you. Have you read what I've written?

MELETUS:
Quite enough of it.

SOCRATES:
Can you tell us where you read that bit about the sun and the moon?

MELETUS:
I'll look it up.

SOCRATES:
I wish you luck, my friend, because I've never written a book. Not even an essay. All I do is talk. *Up:* My fellow Athenians, it's becoming clearer by the minute, you know, that the real heretics here are my accusers. Never mind the Oracle at Delphi — they've invented a riddle of their own: 'Where is the man who believes in gods and believes in no gods at the same time?'

Scorning reply, MELETUS starts to leave the stage. But SOCRATES pounces.

SOCRATES:
Wait! You haven't solved the riddle!

MELETUS: *Flaring.*

You're the riddle-solver here, Socrates. You're the wisest man on earth! The cleverest mind, the cleverest mouth ever known! And you use your cleverness to molest and hurt and confuse decent people who haven't the brains or the training to fight you back. Have you a license to kill others' feelings, and we no license to kill you?   *No reply.*   What gives you the right to play intellectual games with principles the rest of us hold sacred? The Oracle at Delphi? If that's what she meant, where's the riddle! The wisest man on earth ought to be able to get himself out of this little predicament. Think it over. And while you're working on it, do you want me to continue playing goat to your fox?

> *A long pause as they study each other. Finally SOCRATES breaks the eye contact, looks at the assembly, looks at the judges, and turns away. As he does so, he dismisses MELETUS with a weary wave. MELETUS, who can scarcely believe that he has been allowed to have the last word, leaves the stage to rejoin his companions in the front row of the audience.*

SOCRATES:

What am I to say? Am *I* the goat? Hmph.   *He turns frankly and intimately to his audience.*   Knock one of them down and there are two more. Knock three of them down and there are a hundred more. I feel surrounded, standing here. Some of you believe them, no matter what I say. It's this . . . discomfort with what's good, this yearning to hear confirmation of the worst, this goat-song. That's what kills you, in the end. And there's no chance I'd be the last.

> *A dark cloud comes over the assembly as his mood changes. He has, almost suddenly, become older and slower. The ironic shafts, at which he often laughed openly himself, have given way to a kind of bitter earnestness.*

SOCRATES:

There are those who tell me it's no way to live — that I'll come to a bad end, sacrificing everything to an obsession like this. That's what my wife says: 'Why not give it up?' she says. Well, you see, asking the question gives you the answer. If you're going to do something you know is right, then it's wrong to stop on the verge and ask what there's in it for you. If a soldier stopped in battle all the time to calculate his chances of survival, the rest of us mightn't survive at all. And any soldier who got a spear through him while he was flipping a coin could hardly be called a hero. You couldn't even say he died in vain: you'd have to say he miscalculated. It makes no sense to fear death; the thing you need to fear is disgrace. Anyone who's afraid of death is assuming the worst about something he's never met. Who knows? It may be a disaster, it may be the blessing of blessings. But for a soldier under divine command, to disobey an order would certainly be disgraceful. And I'll take possible good over certain evil any time. Wouldn't you?

More breezily.   So! — If you let me go now, don't imagine I'll quit my sentry duty. If these Honourable Judges — *bowing*   — say, 'We'll let you off this time, Socrates, on one condition: that you cut out all this interrogation circus and settle down . . . it's all very interesting, but we really can't have you travelling all over the place infecting young minds, and if we catch you at it again we'll have to put you away for good . . . ' If you put it like that, gentlemen, I'd have to say this. 'Fellow Athenians, I love you! I honour you! But my first allegiance is to the God. And so long as I have life and strength I'll go on cross-examining you, and needling you to examine yourselves, because that is what the God has told me to do! *Someone* has to go around pointing out that real welfare has nothing to do with money or good looks; it depends on what you do to improve your soul. I don't need you half as much as you need me.

Positively heartily: As a matter of fact, I'm the best thing that's ever happened to this city. I'm a God's gift to Athens. I'm a gadfly. A nation is like a horse. — Oh, I know: I don't look like a gadfly and you don't look like a horse, but we are! Athens is a noble stallion that moves so slowly he needs to be stung into action every so often. That's my job. Every day I fasten onto some fat flank and rouse the beast with a well-aimed needle. Of course you resent it! You'll snarl like any hibernator roused from sleep, who spots a gnat and says 'kill the little bugger!' That's what these three worthies would have you do.

31

And then you could all go back to sleep again — unless the gods in their wisdom send you another gadfly. Any volunteers? *Pause.*

Now down to business.   Well. You're going to take a vote, shortly, on my guilt or innocence. That's the first step, and you have only two options: to find me guilty or to acquit me. Now let's suppose I *have* been corrupting the young, as the indictment says. Let's suppose I've been doing it for years — infecting hundreds of young people with my heresies. Wouldn't you expect some of these victims, when they've grown up and realized what poison I fed them — wouldn't you expect them to come out of hiding now and give evidence against me?

Or if they're too shy, what about their outraged relatives — fathers, uncles, brothers, whatever? Why don't they step up and tell the world what a terrible calamity I brought on their houses? Now's the time, my friends: now's the time! I think I see some of you out there. No? What about it, Meletus? Call some witnesses, why don't you? I'll step aside.   *No response.* Is Anytus the only father who objects?   *No response.* Then perhaps that tells you something about who is telling the truth, and who deserves to be acquitted.

Briskly.   What I will not do, even if some of you expect it, is to stage a scene. Don't expect me to clutch my brow and wring out my clothes, or bring my family here to bawl. We've all seen that sort of thing, and naturally it's a very moving experience. Some of you will be offended that I'm not planning an effect of this kind — even though one of the possible penalties, if you find me guilty, is death. I'm not being perverse. I'm human. I have a wife and three sons. But I'm not going to use them to work up sympathy. Parading my human assets before you, as a kind of extenuating circumstance, would be demeaning to them, to me, to you and to Athens. I won't grovel — and that's that.

Having alienated everyone else, he now lectures the Judges.
Anyway, a judge is not supposed to make you a present of justice in return for being worked on; he's supposed to render justice according to the laws of men and gods. Anything else isn't piety, it's perjury. If my plea for acquital could overturn your oaths

to the gods, then I *would* be teaching you the gods are feeble. I'd be perjuring myself, and so would all of you. And we can't have that.

Then, sweetly and confidently, he smiles.   And so to you, my fellow Athenians, and to the God who guides me, I commit my cause, to be judged by you as is best for you — and, I hope, for me.

> *He shrugs, as if to say 'What more can be said?' — and leaves. MELETUS, ANYTUS and LYCON immediately rise from their audience seats and leave together, as the stage lights go down and the house lights come up.*

INTERMISSION

ACT TWO

The platform is bare. Meletus, Anytus and Lycon have gone, their intent fulfilled. Shortly after the lights rise, SOCRATES ambles on, slowly and thoughtfully. But when he looks up, and out at the assembly, he is clearly dangerous.

SOCRATES:

My fellow Athenians. For several reasons, I'm not upset at the guilty verdict. In a way, I expected it. I'm only surprised the vote was so close. Meletus's accusation about atheism hardly carried the fifth of the votes required by law; without Anytus' and Lycon's supporters he'd have had to pay a fine of a thousand drachmas. So it doesn't surprise me that Meletus has asked for the death penalty. He wants a consolation prize, poor fellow. But under our laws I'm allowed to propose my own penalty before you decide on one — although, actually, I'd rather not. If I sentence myself I'm admitting guilt, while to my way of thinking I've won a moral victory.

Well. What's to be my fate. *A topic, not a question.* Obviously you'll have to see that I get my just desserts. The question is: what's just — for an old fart who refuses to join the parade? A man who's never cared a button for comfort, money, power, fame, good times — which are what most of you chase after? Not easy, is it! A man too honest for public life, too generous for private life. A man more concerned about a city on the mend than a city on the make. A man more interested in your souls than in your assets. What do you do for a man like that? If he's going to get his just desserts, my dear fellow countrymen, it ought to be something good. And on top of that, it ought to be appropriate to the man.

Now what sort of reward — we're talking about his sentence — what sort of reward would be appropriate for a man who has everything he wants? — except, of course, leisure: the leisure to kick each and every one of you in the conscience, and open your eyes to your own stupidity. Well, I've mulled it over in the last few minutes, and I can think of only one sentence that fills the bill. Give him a lifetime pension. *He savours the reaction, mock-amazed.* Oh, come now!

Isn't that what you do for Olympic champions, for the muscleman who wins the chariot race? Don't I deserve as much? He gives you an illusion of happiness for a few minutes — I give you the real thing for eternity! Now I ask you: who's the better citizen? In the Athens I know, any man who reaches the top of his profession is loaded with honours and everyone wishes him joy and a long life. In my case you've made an exception. The best gadfly you've ever had is tormented to within an inch of his life. An inch of his life. *Pause.* All in all, it seems to me, anything less than a lifetime pension would be an injustice. *He looks about, innocently.* Do you agree? . . . Can any of you suggest an alternative? . . . One equally — um . . . You don't agree?

Well, I'm certainly not going to find *myself* guilty: 'Socrates, my friend, you've made a mess of it and you deserve to be hung out to dry.' Why should I? Because I'm afraid? Even if I were, which I'm not, you can't back away from injustice merely because your life's at stake. Look . . . *He completely changes his attack, becoming an avuncular and lively story-teller.* I've been on the other side . . .

When I was a Senator — I was, once, you know — only public office I've ever held, right after the battle of Arginusae . . . when we had to try the generals who'd left the bodies rotting on the ground, my clan had the presidency of the Senate, and I was pressed into service. Senator Socrates. Now the assembly — all you people, or your parents or grandparents — wanted to try the generals in a batch, which everyone admitted afterwards went clean against the law. I was the only one of the Judges, my friends — the only one — who had the guts to vote against you! Eh? What about that! *He laughs, pointing at the present Judges.* I stood up to everybody! And when the lawyers for the generals tried to have me impeached, you egged them on! You did! You did! *He laughs hugely at the memory.*

35

What a pack of lemmings!   *Sobering:*   Two days later,
everyone had to admit I was right and they were wrong.
So . . . that was when I made up my mind . . . that as long as
justice and the law were on my side, I'd face prison, I'd face
death — but I'd never juggle with my own soul. That's the one
option you *know* is bad.

Reasonably.   Of course, I could suggest exile. Exile would
be honourable, it's a popular penalty, and it would save my skin.
I'm sure some of you would find it highly appropriate for a
gadfly: shoo him out of the house. But what good would that
do? Do you honestly think I'd stand a chance as a sort of roving
outcast? If my fellow Athenians find my hectoring so
objectionable, are others more likely to lap it up? Can you
imagine the life I'd lead, at my age, wandering from city to city
and being thrown out of one place after another like a mangy
cur? Wherever I'd go it'd be the same story. The young fellows
would flock to hear me; if I turned them away they'd resent it
and tell their fathers, and the fathers would see I was moved
on. If I agreed to take them on, the fathers would be after me
for that. It might be a far worse fate than death — and anyway,
death's bound to find me before long, wherever I go. Unless any
of you happen to know a place outside the city limits where death
never comes . . .   *He pauses for a moment — not in expectation
of a reply, but because he has answered his own question; it is as if he
now sees his audience as separate individuals, not as a mob.*

I'm saying all this badly. I know some of you want to help.
'Socrates,' I can imagine one of you saying, 'Socrates, old boy,
why can't you for God's sake hold your tongue! If only you'd
swallow your home truths instead of spitting them in people's
faces, you could go anywhere in the world without let or
hindrance.' That sort of thing. Well, the explanation, the reason
I can't, is deeply personal. It really is 'for God's sake' that I
must not hold my tongue. The fact is, the choice isn't mine to
make.   *And he becomes quietly confessional.*

You've heard me speak, some of you, from time to time — some
of my friends have — of a sort of inner voice that talks to me.
It's . . . it's the divine sign that Meletus was poking fun at —
and it's true. This voice, this small irresistible voice, started

coming to me when I was a child. And it sounds odd, I know, but it never commands me to *do* anything; it only warns me *against* doing something — something I'm thinking of doing but know I shouldn't. It was my voice that kept me out of politics. People used to ask me why I didn't run for office, help set policy, give the government the benefit of my advice instead of carping from the sidelines. The government, after all, could do wholesale what I've been doing piecemeal for our young people. Very tempting. But my voice said 'No.' And I had to lie low and work away like a mole.

But when it came to the God's mission, when it came to finding out why the God said there was no man wiser than Socrates — which on the face of it was ridiculous — my little voice said nothing. Not a word. And I knew I was on the right track.   *Sailing, his sails billowing with enthusiasm.*   Making people think, really think . . . about the *point* of life, about the point of their own lives . . . getting them to examine, each of them, their potential as human beings — that's the highest calling a man can have! But if I say to you now, as I've said again and again, that the unexamined life is not worth living — and even though I'm desperately trying to set an example — you'll probably pay no more attention than you ever have. You'll all go on, just as you have before, thinking you need no Socrates to tell you what the God has told him.   *Pause.*   And if I've failed the God in any way, it's that I can't seem to make his truth more palatable — not, at least, it seems, to most of you, and to these Honourable Judges.   *He stops, driven by the last point to wonder about a compromise.*

Thinking aloud.   If I had any money, of course, I might let us all off the hook by proposing a fine. I might estimate the value of the offense, in the light of what I could afford to pay. It wouldn't be much, but you'd get your penalty and I'd get my reprimand. But the fact is I have no money. Haven't had for years. I've let everything slide while I worked for you, trying to knock some sense into your silly heads. My sort of behavior, you know, isn't exactly normal, so I don't have a normal income. In their wildest slanders, my accusers never suggest I take a pittance from anyone. My poverty is the proof of my innocence. I've saved nothing. My purse is flat. And the only thing I can suggest is that you make the fine fit the purse: flat.

Mock astonishment.   Is that completely outrageous? Well, I suppose I . . . I don't know; perhaps . . . I really can't afford

37

it, you know, but — if it's better than nothing — I'll propose a fine of one mina. *Pause.* No? . . . Unacceptable? . . . Thirty, Plato? *Shrugging as if to say 'I hope you know what you're doing'* Thank you, Plato . . . Crito . . . thank you, Critobulus, thanks Apollodorus. Honourable Judges, my friends want me to say thirty minas. I don't have it . . . I can only think they mean to underwrite a loan. Well, if they're willing, so am I. I propose a fine of thirty minas. *Pause: then, ingenuously.* So you have a choice now. A genuine choice. I'm at your disposal.

Bowing respectfully to the Judges, SOCRATES walks briskly off, as the lights dim slightly to denote a short passage of time.

The lights rise once more, on an empty platform. A pause. Then SOCRATES returns, this time gravely. He stands a moment, surveying the assembly.

SOCRATES:

Well . . . my fellow Athenians . . . you think you have bought some time. Not much, I'm afraid, when you consider the cost. Hardly a bargain: my life in exchange for a black eye. Every foreigner who wants to knock Athens can hold up the caricature you've just drawn of yourselves with your own hand. 'The Athenians killed Socrates, the wisest man in Athens' — that's what they'll say. I'm not wise, of course — except in the sense we've been talking about — but they'll say I am, just to get at you. And all for what? If you'd waited a little while, Nature would have done it for you. It's pretty obvious I'm on my last legs. *A thought.* I'm not saying this to everyone here, you know — only to whom it may concern: those of you who got impatient.

I know others mean well. Some of you with kind intentions, perhaps, see capital punishment as hard but fair — fair under the circumstances, because I never hit on the right tactics to get around it. I didn't explore all the legal loopholes. You're wrong, you know. The missing ingredient wasn't a piece of legal hocus-pocus. It was a *performance*! When the time came, I was myself. I can never be anything else. I didn't act like a protagonist out of Sophocles — up on my high boots, bellowing like a prize bull, embracing my hypothetical widow and orphans, tears of blood running down my mask. That's not my style. That's not me. Do you know what was going through my head, instead, at that moment? — That I would never, no matter what the provocation, make a spectacle of myself and drag my family into it, just because my life was at stake.

Philosophically.   I'll tell you plainly, the trick is not to avoid death — you can't. It's to avoid doing wrong — because wrong will catch up with you first. I'm old and slow now, and the slower · runner has overtaken me. My accusers are much younger than I am, full of piss and vinegar, but the mischief they've done has caught up with them already. That's all right. I'm leaving here under sentence of death, and they're going off under sentence of conscience. I'm happy with my lot: I hope they're happy with theirs.

He turns hard.   But none of you can afford to feel superior — to me or to them. As soon as I've gone, you're going to be inflicted with a far worse punishment than you've inflicted on me. You want to finish me off so you can carry on as before, with no final reckoning to face. Well, think again. Before long, you'll have more accusers than I've had today. I'm talking about *my* generation, the next generation — and they'll be hard on you, and you will hate it. But if you think getting rid of me will clear the way for you to carry on again, shaming the human spirit, living out your shabby lives with no notion of what you're doing, you can expect a shock. That is not a real option. The answer is not to push somebody else down but to lift yourselves up!   *He shrugs as if to say I pity you, then becomes very tender.*

I can't leave without saying something to those of you who wanted to acquit me. Wait a moment . . .   *To the Judges.*   May we have a little time? . . . Thank you.

To one group: My friends, I have something wonderful to tell you. Up to now, my little voice has always sounded an alarm when I was in danger of taking a wrong step. Well, here I am; I've just tripped over the steepest step of all — and my voice said nothing. Not when I left the house this morning, not when I got into court, not while I was speaking. It's often brought me up short in mid-sentence, you know — but today there was nothing I did or said that set off that alarm. The only explanation is that there is no cause for alarm. That death is good and that people who think it's evil are dead wrong. Otherwise, you see, the voice would have told me.

But I've other reasons for thinking I'm on the right track. There are really only two possibilities: that death is an ending, like a light going out, or a transition, a sort of flight from one world to the next. Assume, for instance, that when you die you lose consciousness, go into a kind of eternal sleep — no dreams, even. Then obviously death is a great blessing: eternity is a single night.

But take the alternative: that death is the gateway to another place — a place where the souls of the dead live on. Could you ask for anything better? You arrive in the next world, fresh from an encounter with what passes for justice in this one, to be greeted by the wisest judges in all creation. Now I'd call that progress! *Soaring:* Imagine: hobnobbing with all the great men who've been wrongfully put to death . . . discussing the merits of capital punishment with the experts: those who've been through it . . . and continuing my search with all of humanity as my sample! Finding out who's wise and who's a fool, quizzing Agamemnon and Odysseus and Homer, arguing and nattering with anyone I please! *He becomes aware of the larger audience, and raises his voice: it breaks.* It's only in this world that they put you to death for asking questions!

For a moment his bravado slips; he recovers. All right. *To the whole assembly:* I'm all right! *He collects himself and resumes the ironic note.* When I've drunk the hemlock, I'll be in heaven. Not from the taste. Before I go I'd like to thank those of you who've sent me there by condemning me today. *With a triumphant smile.* You didn't know what you were doing — you certainly didn't think you were doing me a favour! — but that's the way of it. Nothing bad can happen to a good man; the gods don't let him die by accident. They may see that you get what's coming to you, but it won't be my affair. *He laughs ruefully.* I won't be here to help you, my fellow Athenians! — my Honourable Judges! *Bows.* But I wish you all the luck you are going to need.

He starts to leave, but suddenly stops, listening internally.
What? . . . Not yet? . . . Oh yes. Of course.   *He turns back,*
looking out over the audience.   I'd like to ask a favour of my
friends — Plato and the rest of you: you who earlier offered to
help me. When my three sons have grown up, keep them in line.
Their mother, God love her, can only do so much, and I've left
her nothing to do it on. Go after those boys, my friends, as I've
gone after you, if they fall in love with money or anything else
that drives the wits out of their heads. And if they pretend to
be something they aren't, kick their shins, as I did yours, until
they take a good look at themselves. If you do this, we'll have
had justice, I and my family, from the people of Athens.

That's really all I have to say. Are the proceedings over? Then
that's that. Time for us to go. I'm going to die, you're going
to live. Only a God knows which is better.

> *But he does not go. Instead, he stands, uncertainly, listening intently*
> *to an inner prompting, as if he were being reminded of something*
> *left unsaid. The lights fade to black.*

CURTAIN

THE STORE

a play in one act

Persons in the play:
　　The Manager
　　The Woman
　　The Assistant Manager
　　The Secretary

The present version of "The Store" was first produced by the Canadian Broadcasting Corporation in 1971, in an adaptation for the television series "Program X," produced by George Jonas. It was directed by Herb Roland, with Joseph Shaw as the Manager and Barbara Hamilton as the Woman.

The office of the Manager of a large department store. The essential elements are his large desk, on which stands an intercom box along with telephones, and the usual desk accoutrements including an elaborate letter knife; a stuffed owl which sits atop a filing cabinet in a corner; his desk chair and two others facing him for visitors; and the single entrance door.

Whenever the door is opened we hear the clamour from the store: busy crowds of shoppers, cash register bells, etc. — and whenever the door is shut it ceases abruptly. As the house lights dim, we hear the clamour. It comes up full in the darkness, then fades out as the stage lighting comes up. The door is shut.

The Manager is seated at his desk, a pile of papers in his hand. Standing facing him is the Assistant Manager. The Manager is outwardly a very solid, commanding executive without a trace of the neurotic even when angry — which he is at the moment. The Assistant is a harried man who has risen within the firm by being a faithful servant.

MANAGER:
Complaints! Complaints! Complaints! Can't you bring me anything but complaints?

ASSISTANT:
I'm very sorry, sir —

MANAGER:
What's an assistant manager for if he can't assistant manage?

ASSISTANT:
But sir, this clergyman was irate. He invoked Jesus Christ several times.

MANAGER:
It won't do him any good. The discount for clerics has been discontinued, and that's that.

ASSISTANT:
He says the whole moral order of man is disintegrating.

MANAGER:

Let him! That's his job. It's our job to look after the store. And the way men are messing things up, these days, we've both got our work cut out for us.

ASSISTANT: *Going to the door.*
Yes sir. I'll tell him that. *He opens the door.*

MANAGER: *Turning away.*
That'll be all, Mr. Pontifex.

While Pontifex is at the door, and unseen by the Manager, the Woman slips into the office, ending up behind and beyond Pontifex.

ASSISTANT:

Yes sir. I'll try not to interrupt unless it's something essential. *He goes, closing the door behind him. The Manager drops with fatigue. Then he flicks on the intercom.*

SECRETARY: *Female, over intercom.*
Yes sir?

MANAGER:

Miss Chang, I am not to be disturbed. Please hold all calls unless they're urgent.

SECRETARY:
Yes sir.

He flicks off the intercom. Then he girds his loins, picks up a pen and starts to check off a list of items on his desk. Angrily he crumples one and throws it in the wastebasket.

The Woman steps forward. She is middle-aged, overdressed, aggressive and clearly unbalanced. The Manager, on the other hand, is just as clearly in command of the situation.

WOMAN:
I want to see the manager, please.

46

MANAGER:
How did you —

WOMAN:
I've been waiting for a long time, and I want to see the manager.

MANAGER: *Rising.*
I am the manager, madam.

WOMAN:
Then you're the person I want to see.

MANAGER:
I thought as much. *His habitual diplomatic manner winning out, he comes forward and shifts a chair for her.* What can I do for you? Please sit down.

WOMAN: *Sitting by the desk.*
I have a complaint to make.

MANAGER: *Returning to his chair.*
Naturally.

WOMAN:
It isn't natural at all. I don't go round making complaints.

MANAGER:
I didn't mean to imply —

WOMAN:
I only bitch when there's something to bitch about. Generally I'm a very good-natured person.

MANAGER:
Naturally.

WOMAN:
But this time I intend to raise an old-fashioned stink.

MANAGER:
Naturally.

WOMAN:

Is that a tic you have, or do you keep saying that because your customers are always complaining?

MANAGER:

Not at all. That wouldn't be wise, even if it were true. I only meant —

WOMAN:

It wouldn't surprise me. Your clerks are snippy; rude, even.

MANAGER:

We do our best to —

WOMAN:

There's no use taking a complaint to them — all you get is the runaround. It's always the customer who's wrong. And so high and mighty!

MANAGER:

It's hard to keep good clerks these days.

WOMAN:

Oh, that's always the excuse! What's so different about these days? — unless it's that you ought to be able to get better ones. As long as I can remember —

MANAGER: *Smoothly.*

Not long, madam, I'm sure.

WOMAN:

Oh, bull! Don't soft soap me: it won't work. Why should I waste time with their nonsense? My time is valuable.

MANAGER:

We have a complaint department.

WOMAN:

Nothing but soft soap. So I've gone over their heads, and I expect some straight talk.

MANAGER:
>
> That's always the customer's privilege. Now what seems to be the trouble?

Throughout her story he remains impassive, toying with a letter knife.

WOMAN:
>
> It began with the owl and the skunk. I was walking home through the woods, after cutting off juniper roots with the clippers, when I stepped right into a skunk, lying across the path in a pool of blood and stuck all over with owl feathers. I stood there in a kind of spell — it was so unnatural, an owl going after a skunk like that! I must have aged ten years. Finally I got away, and raced along the path to the house. I shouted for my father and my mother, but there was no answer. I dashed through every room, upstairs, downstairs. In the kitchen, the sink was piled high with broken plates and silver, all covered with green mould. Decent silver shouldn't go like that. Upstairs in the back bedroom I shared with my older sister, I found her lying across the bed, strangled by a leather belt. I hope you're noting these things: belts do a lot more than hold up whatever it is. In the front bedroom I found my mother, looking terribly old. She'd been done in with an ice-pick. I've never had anything to do with ice-picks since. It was getting dark, and downstairs again I lit a candle: left it there while I ran out to the barn, looking for my father. A cry from the empty house made me turn — it was my father's voice. The house was in flames — it must have been the candle — and try as I would I couldn't make my way in. In a few moments it was all gone: the house, the bodies, the barn, the animals, my father . . .
>
> It was on that account that I ran away and married the first man I met — a buyer for this store, who drank to excess. And when he mercifully died in a car crash due to defective brakes. — No: that was my second husband; my first was electrocuted trying to fix the oven — I had only one thing left in life, my children: a fine boy and a lovely girl. I was forced to go to work; took training as a computer programmer, where I learned that what comes out is only what you put in, if you follow me. It's all there on the cards. Six months ago, while I was out working, my darling son was suffocated in the refrigerator. Yesterday my daughter was horribly disfigured by an accident with her electric toothbrush. Now: what are you going to do about it?

MANAGER:
    Yes. Well . . .

On his desk, the intercom buzzes.

MANAGER:
    Excuse me.   *He drops the knife, flicks on the intercom.*   Yes?

SECRETARY: *Over intercom.*
    Mr. Fitzroy from the drug department's on the line . . .

MANAGER:
    Can't he handle it? — I'm tied up at the moment.

SECRETARY:
    It's that Virox B again.

MANAGER:
    What about it?

SECRETARY:
    Seven more male customers with hair growing inside the scalp
    — they've gone insane.

MANAGER:
    Refer them to the manufacturer.

SECRETARY:
    I'll tell him.

MANAGER: *Switching off intercom.*
    Now then, we were talking about a defective toothbrush?

WOMAN:
    Oh, you can't skip out of it as easily as that.

MANAGER:
    But I thought you said —

WOMAN:
    You're responsible for the whole thing.

50

MANAGER:
I'm not sure I understand you.

WOMAN:
Everything. You're responsible for everything.

MANAGER: *Smoothly.*
Possibly — but we're discussing liability, surely. Not quite the same —

WOMAN:
And you think that after all I've been through I'll settle for a measly toothbrush?

MANAGER:
The settlement may depend on any injury suffered, of course, but beyond that . . .

WOMAN:
Any?   *Starting to weep.*   *Every* injury, from start to finish!   *She extracts a handkerchief from her purse and weeps into it.*   Oh, you're brutes! Power-mad brutes!

A pause while he comes around his desk to sit on a chair near her.

MANAGER:
You know, I'm very sympathetic, Mrs. —?

WOMAN:
Moffat.

MANAGER:
Yours is a terrible story, Mrs. Moffat . . .

WOMAN:
It isn't a story. I didn't make up a word of it.

MANAGER:
. . . almost a nightmare, one might say. Something . . . irrational.

WOMAN:

What's irrational about it? That sort of thing happens — or did happen, or could happen.

MANAGER:

We seem to be a little confused.

WOMAN:

You may be — I'm not.

MANAGER:

Now look here, Mrs. Moffat: we're not concerned with what *might* happen — let's get that quite clear. Sympathy is one thing but business another. We must deal with a specific event which can be proved to have happened. Our liability doesn't extend to —

WOMAN:

How can you say that when it's perfectly obvious they're all connected? If it has happened it can happen, and if it can happen it will! And if it happens, you're responsible.

MANAGER:

I fail to see, madam —

> *The door opens. The Assistant Manager enters, closing the door behind him. He ignores Mrs. Moffat completely.*

ASSISTANT:

Sorry to interrupt, but there's a man out here being very abusive. Claims his boy blew himself up with one of our toy rockets.

MANAGER:

Will they never learn?

ASSISTANT:

I've already sent him to the legal department. They say it's in your hands.

MANAGER:

Oh yes! It's always . . . Get the details, Mr. Pontifex, and tell him it's in my hands.

ASSISTANT:
Right.

The Assistant Manager leaves, closing the door behind him.

WOMAN:
Well, what did I tell you!

MANAGER: *Ignoring the taunt.*
. . . Now where were we? Ah yes: was this toothbrush a cash
purchase or do you have a charge account?

WOMAN:
I always pay cash; I don't believe in incurring obligations.

MANAGER:
If you had had a charge account —

WOMAN:
My family's dealt with this store for three generations — I'm
no casual shopper.

MANAGER:
It's a matter of how this particular purchase —

WOMAN:
We're not talking about one little item like a toothbrush, you
know; get *that* straight! We're talking about years and years of
incompetence and inefficiency, a whole funeral of duds and frosts
and swindles . . .

MANAGER:
Our firm's good name, Mrs. Moffat —

WOMAN:
. . . Breakdown is your middle name!

MANAGER:
Mrs. Moffat, *all* appliances break down sooner or later! In time,
everything disintegrates, or almost everything.

WOMAN:

Is that an excuse to put out fiascos in the first place?

MANAGER:

Every piece of merchandise that leaves this store is tested in our laboratories and workshops. Every effort is made to —

WOMAN:

To prevent what *might* happen?

MANAGER: *Emphatically.*

To see that our products function properly — that is the extent of our responsibility. For that we have guarantees, warranties. *Wheeling on her.* Did you have a warranty on that toothbrush?

WOMAN:

The toothbrush, the toothbrush! We'll start at the beginning, if you don't mind, not at the end.

MANAGER:

At the beginning of what?

WOMAN:

Every unnatural thing that has happened in my life is a direct result of some disaster put out by you — and I want compensation.

MANAGER: *Hitting the roof.*

In all my life —

WOMAN:

We haven't time for that now.

MANAGER: *Winding up and finally exploding.*

No matter what you have been told, Mrs. Moffat, I am not the First Cause!

WOMAN:

Then who is?

MANAGER:

I've been blamed, eternally, for every malfeasance of man, let alone every natural disaster, and even for causing the latter as punishment for the former.

WOMAN:

Sounds to me as if you hadn't the faintest idea *what* you were doing.

MANAGER:

I'm sick and tired of being made the goat for every trip and stumble of every Tom, Dick and Betty who are perfectly free to buy whatever they want to, and not buy whatever they don't want — foul the thing up and then blame the thing instead of their own ineptitude!

WOMAN:

If you're sick and tired you oughtn't to be in this job — and you won't put me off with a recital of *your* troubles. I'm here about mine.

MANAGER:

Madam, your troubles are my troubles.

WOMAN:

They certainly are! Or at any rate they certainly will be if I don't get satisfaction. The whole thing began —

MANAGER: *Controlling himself.*

Very well. Let us go from the beginning of your story.

WOMAN:

That's what I said in the first place.

MANAGER: *Fresh attack: being immensely reasonable.*

It began, I think you said, with, some years ago, an owl attacking a skunk. Most unnatural, I agree. But Mrs. Moffat, we have never sold live animals — not wild ones, at any rate: that is the whole point of their being wild. If someone were responsible for their behaviour —

WOMAN:

You can't get out of it that way. I would have arrived there in time to prevent it if your clippers had been working properly.

MANAGER:

Clippers?

WOMAN:

I knew you weren't taking it in. That's what kept me so long cutting juniper roots. If I'd come along earlier it would never have happened; I'd have gone straight home and got there in time to —

MANAGER:

Now just a moment: juniper roots have nothing —

WOMAN:

Those were your dishes in the sink . . .

MANAGER:

What?

WOMAN:

That was your belt my sister was strangled with . . .

MANAGER:

Oh really —!

WOMAN:

Your tethers on the horses . . .

MANAGER:

The tethers were in no way connected —

WOMAN:

And if your defective candle hadn't fallen over, or whatever it did, the house would never have burned down with everybody in it, and I wouldn't have had to run away and marry the first fool I met.

MANAGER:
Are you suggesting —

WOMAN:
It was working at this store that drove him to drink. The stove that did him in, drunk as he was, came from this place.

MANAGER:
The alcohol too, I presume!

WOMAN:
The car whose faulty brakes killed my second husband was serviced at your garage. The refrigerator —

MANAGER:
Stop!

WOMAN:
The toothbrush —

MANAGER:
Stop! Now look here, Mrs. Moffat: beyond refunding your money for goods found unsatisfactory, this firm has no liability unless you can prove that any damages you suffered were caused by our negligence.

WOMAN:
Negligence is your middle name.

MANAGER:
No company can be held responsible for outright misuse of its products. It's absurd! A bathtub can kill you if you step on a bar of soap.

WOMAN:
Don't change the subject. The clippers first.

MANAGER:
If the clippers were not functioning properly you should have done something about it at the time.

WOMAN:

A little girl? A homeless orphan?

MANAGER:

Then you should have taken some action as soon as you could, not years later when the evidence has gone up in smoke, nothing can be checked . . . A candle! — What nonsense!

WOMAN:

It only makes sense when you look at it backwards, not forwards.

MANAGER:

Now really!

WOMAN:

I had to wait until I knew. How could I do anything about anything until I knew what it was all about?

MANAGER:

At this rate we'd never —

WOMAN:

It's only now I can see how it all fits . . . how my troubles began with your clippers.

MANAGER:

No, they did not. Before then, unhappily, you were conceived, born . . .

WOMAN:

But they were the first sign, the first omen. I can only go by what I remember . . .

MANAGER:

I'm afraid that's not good enough for us.

WOMAN:

. . . and by what I foresee.

MANAGER:

Madam, for the last time, we do not deal in signs, omens,

auguries or premonitions. That is what things may become for certain people, perhaps, after they leave these premises, but —

WOMAN:
You're not responsible?

MANAGER:
For your whole life?

WOMAN:
For my death.

The intercom buzzes.

MANAGER: *Going to the desk.*
Excuse me.   *He flicks it on.*   Yes?

SECRETARY: *Over intercom.*
Excuse me, but the deputation from the Consumers' Association has arrived.

MANAGER:
What deputation?

SECRETARY:
About the rain-making machines.

MANAGER:
I've already told them we give no guarantee with our rain-makers!

SECRETARY:
But what am I to do with them?

MANAGER:
Do what you like! Give them hoses, watering cans — make water! — But please do not disturb me again!   *Switches off intercom.*

WOMAN:
Watering cans!

MANAGER:

Now then, Mrs. Moffat, let us get down to brass tacks. Do you have the bills for these various transactions?

WOMAN:

No.

MANAGER:

Then how can we —

WOMAN:

I trusted you.

MANAGER:

Surely you realize that without the bills we are not liable in any way for merchandise you claim to have purchased at this store. Furthermore —

WOMAN:

But I did.

MANAGER:

Mrs. Moffat, I have been very patient. We are always willing to help our clients, but I must make it clear that without the bill whatever we do is a matter of goodwill on our part, and in no way a legal obligation. It is possible the transactions can be traced: we shall do our best. *Sits and prepares to take notes.* Now: rather than start at the beginning, if you don't mind, we'll start with the most recent transaction, since you'll be better able to recall the details.

WOMAN:

It doesn't matter where you start, it's where you end up — and that's not the end.

MANAGER:

Nevertheless. *Makes notes.* Toothbrush. What was the girl's name?

WOMAN:

Edwards.

MANAGER:
> No, the girl's.

WOMAN:
> Elizabeth Edwards.

MANAGER:
> . . . Moffat.

WOMAN:
> No, Edwards — my second husband.

MANAGER:
> I see. And when did you buy it: do you recall?

WOMAN:
> About a month ago.

MANAGER:
> About?

WOMAN:
> Give or take a couple of weeks.

MANAGER:
> Have you any idea of our volume of sales, Mrs. Moffat? — of how many electric toothbrushes we sell every day?

WOMAN:
> You shouldn't be selling them at all.

MANAGER:
> You are not forced to buy. Let me remind you that I'm doing you a favour in looking into this at all!   *Pause.*   We only carry on our shelves what people will purchase, and we carry what people want whether we happen to want to or not. Personally I regard electric toothbrushes as worse than unnecessary — I regard them as dangerous; but so long as people continue to buy them, then we will continue to sell them, putting out the best and safest product we can. Now: how did she injure herself?

WOMAN:
I'd rather not say.

MANAGER:
Did she see a dentist?

WOMAN:
Why should she see a dentist?

MANAGER:
In order to determine the form of injury.

WOMAN:
Oh, for heaven's sake, anyone could tell!

MANAGER:
Well, will someone tell? Were there any witnesses?

WOMAN:
Certainly not!

MANAGER:
This is impossible. What about the refrigerator: when was it
purchased?

WOMAN:
About three years ago.

MANAGER:
Now surely you can do better than that! *He begins to circle
her, notebook at the ready.* Think back, Mrs. Moffat. Where
did you live at the time? What were you doing then? Wasn't
there something unusual that happened just before you purchased
the refrigerator, or just after? Now think.

WOMAN:
I'm thinking.

MANAGER:
Ah, now we're getting somewhere. Now we're being
constructive. Well?

WOMAN:
 I can't remember.

MANAGER:
 Think! Go back, Mrs. Moffat! Think back!

WOMAN:
 I can't remember when I try to remember things out of order!

MANAGER:
 But you're asking *me* to remember things out of order! Millions of sales a day, and you expect —

WOMAN:
 I told you to begin at the beginning! One thing comes after another, and makes you remember the thing after that — it's no use trying to do it all mixed up!

MANAGER:
 I'm trying to make it easy for you, Mrs. Moffat, not trying to mix you up! Come now: isn't there *something* that can jog your memory? Some domestic crisis? A new dress? Some wedding or birth or death to which you could attach a date? Some *other* accident? Some epidemic? Some national or international event: an election, a revolution, a landing on the moon?

WOMAN:
 Wait a minute . . .

MANAGER:
 Yes?

WOMAN:
 Our rabbit had bunnies, which the father ate.

MANAGER:
 Not, unfortunately, recorded in the newspapers. Think again, Mrs. Moffat. I must warn you that your life depends on your ability to establish that the merchandise concerned was purchased in this store, and that we were in some way negligent.

WOMAN:

It killed my boy!

MANAGER:

A machine is not a person, Mrs. Moffat: it does only what it is programmed to do. People have freedom of will; a machine —

WOMAN:

He didn't lock *himself* inside!

MANAGER:

It is unnatural for refrigerators to kill people; they are designed to keep food cold.

WOMAN:

Whatever they can do they will!

MANAGER:

That again! This store, madam, is not responsible for the conduct of an appliance led astray by someone ignorant of its proper use! And we have not yet even established that it was one of ours!

WOMAN:

Would I be here if it weren't?

MANAGER:

That is exactly what we have to establish. If you can't remember what happened three years ago, how can we possibly go back ten, twenty —

WOMAN:

It was Thursday, November the eighteenth, at half-past eleven.

MANAGER: *After a long look at her.*

All right. What was the boy's name.

WOMAN:

Betti.

MANAGER:

The boy?

WOMAN:
By my first husband: Arturo Betti. B-E-T-T-I.

MANAGER:
That's the husband's name?

WOMAN:
No, the boy's.

MANAGER:
And also your name at the time of purchase?

WOMAN:
No, Edwards.

MANAGER:
Who was electrocuted by the oven.

WOMAN:
No, that was Betti.

The door opens and shuts. The Assistant Manager enters. As before, he ignores Mrs. Moffat.

ASSISTANT:
I'm terribly sorry to interrupt, but the delivery drivers have gone on strike.

MANAGER:
Can't you see I'm busy. Mr. Pontifex?

ASSISTANT:
They're complaining about hours, working conditions, pay . . .

MANAGER:
Complaints, complaints, complaints! What's the matter with our Industrial Relations office?

ASSISTANT:
They've gone on strike too. You've got to take a hand — everything's breaking down!

MANAGER:
Then fix it! I am not to be disturbed! Get out!

ASSISTANT:
Yes sir.

The door opens and closes as he goes. The Manager locks the door after him.

WOMAN: *Taunting.*
Breakdown . . . Breakdown!

MANAGER:
Now, Mrs. Moffat, let us come to grips. Your son Arturo Betti, you say, locked himself in one of our refrigerators, purchased three years ago at 11:30 A.M. on Thursday, November 18th, and suffocated. How old was he?

WOMAN:
Twenty-seven.

MANAGER: *Incredulous.*
At the time he died?

WOMAN:
Well, if he hasn't already, he will do.

MANAGER:
I suspected as much. We're dealing with hypothetical events, aren't we, Mrs. Moffat!

WOMAN:
I don't know what you mean.

MANAGER:
None of these things ever really happened, did they?

WOMAN:
You can't get out of it that way — by pretending things don't go wrong! If they can they will!

MANAGER:
But in these particular instances —

WOMAN:
We haven't finished yet . . .

MANAGER:
We certainly haven't — and we're going to if it takes —

WOMAN:
Go back to the beginning and you'll see we've not finished yet!

MANAGER:
We've hardly begun, have we? The clippers, the belt, the candle — when were they purchased, and by whom?

WOMAN:
My father, when I was a child.

MANAGER:
And the name?

WOMAN:
Svidrigailov.

MANAGER:
Four names. Four different names you've been shopping under at this store, Mrs. Moffat: Moffat, Edwards, Betti and now Svidrigailov! You deliberately set out to confuse us, didn't you?

WOMAN:
No!

MANAGER:
. . . Deliberately set out to shift the blame onto us for your own nightmares!

WOMAN:
No!

MANAGER: *Low and knowing.*
  You never had a daughter, did you, Mrs. Moffat?

WOMAN:
  What?

MANAGER:
  It was you yourself who used the toothbrush, improperly, if I
  may say so, hoping that by sympathetic magic —

WOMAN:
  That's a lie!

MANAGER:
  And your son: your son was born prematurely, wasn't he!

WOMAN:
  What's that got to do with it?

MANAGER:
  Locked in the fridge, indeed! And the car whose defective brakes
  caused, or might cause, or may cause the death of your second
  husband — or was it, or will it be, your first? — you wanted
  him to go on and on and on, never to stop —

WOMAN:
  You killed him!

MANAGER:
  I killed a figment of *your* imagination?

WOMAN:
  No, no!

MANAGER:
  And the other husband, the one who was or will be electrocuted
  trying to fix the oven . . . is there a death certificate?

WOMAN:
  Unnatural causes . . . unnatural causes!

MANAGER:
They never existed, did they!

WOMAN:
Yes!

MANAGER:
If they existed, Mrs. Moffat, who killed them, eh? Who was it who wanted these inept mechanics out of the way? And why? I suggest to you . . .

WOMAN:
It was an accident!

MANAGER:
Come now, Mrs. Moffat, there are no accidents in your life, are there? Isn't it all in the cards? Doesn't what can happen happen?

WOMAN:
It *all* happened! My mother, my sister —

MANAGER:
Your father too?

WOMAN:
Yes, my father!

MANAGER:
Your father was real, was alive . . .

WOMAN:
Yes!

MANAGER:
Alive when the others were dead: is that it?

WOMAN:
He was killed in the fire made by that candle of yours!

MANAGER:
Was it our candle or his you blame?

69

WOMAN:
Yours! There was nothing left!

MANAGER:
Nothing found, you mean. Shall I tell you how it happened, Mrs. Moffat? An owl, driven to unnatural deeds by a tormenting skunk, lay in your path as you were returning home, armed with a root clipper. It delayed you, whether ten minutes or ten years is no matter. When you arrived home, it was to find your sister and your mother murdered, and your father gone. You yourself set fire to the house —

WOMAN:
No: I was out in the barn!

MANAGER:
Looking for your father! If only you could have used those clippers! You hated your father, didn't you, for murdering your mother, your sister — for abandoning you, for —

WOMAN:
My whole life —

MANAGER:
Yes, all of it! Your whole life you want to lay at my door! Grudges and grievances, hates and complaints, all that happened and could happen and might happen . . .

WOMAN: *A cry.*
They were real! Everything was real!

MANAGER: *His hands at her throat.*
As real, Mrs. Moffat, as you are to me.

WOMAN:
Get away from me . . .

MANAGER:
Putting it all on the store . . .

WOMAN:
I'll raise a stink! . . .

MANAGER:
Lies and darkness . . .

WOMAN:
Treating customers like animals . . .

MANAGER: *Pulling at her purse as she struggles free.*
You buy this here? *Snatching it.* We'll take it back!

WOMAN:
Thieves! Robbers!

MANAGER:
And this? *Her coat.* Any complaints? *He pulls
it off her.* We'll take it back!

WOMAN:
Help! Help! Somebody help me! *She reaches for the intercom:
in preventing her, the Manager switches it on.* Help! Help
me! *She disengages.*

MANAGER: *Grabbing her and tearing her dress.*
This defective too?

SECRETARY: *Voice from box, continuing under dialogue from here
to the end.*
May I help you? . . . Yes sir? . . . May I help you? . . . Were
you calling? . . . Hello! . . . Is anyone there? . . . Hello! . . .
May I help you? . . . Hello! Hello! . . . Were you calling,
sir? . . . May I help you? . . .

WOMAN:
No! *She flails back at him.*

MANAGER:
Bitch! *Strikes her.*

WOMAN:
　　Stop! Stop!

MANAGER:
　　No, go back! Back!　　　　*Strikes her.*

　　　　Pounding on the door, continues.

ASSISTANT:　　　　*Outside the door, under stage action.*
　　Is anything the matter? . . . What's going on in there? . . .
　　Open the door! . . . What's going on? . . . Open up! . . .
　　What's happening in there? . . . Somebody get a key! . . .
　　What's wrong? . . . Open up! . . . Open the door!

　　　　Mrs. Moffat fights free and reaches for the letter knife on the desk.
　　　　They wrestle for it. She is forced to the floor. He takes the knife,
　　　　as if to an animal, and plunges it into her three times.

MANAGER:
　　Bitch! Bitch! Bitch!

　　　　She subsides with a moan. He kneels beside her, panting. The door
　　　　burst open and the Assistant Manager stands there. He ignores Mrs.
　　　　Moffat. The voice of the secretary from the intercom continues in
　　　　the background.

ASSISTANT:　　　　*At door.*
　　Are you all right sir?

MANAGER:　　　　*Slowly, mechanically: an owl.*
　　Who?

ASSISTANT:
　　You, sir.

MANAGER:
　　No . . . complaints. I've killed them all.　　　*Pause.*　　　Get
　　her out of here.

ASSISTANT:
　　Who, sir?

MANAGER:
> On the path . . . the skunk.

ASSISTANT: *Advancing.*
> A skunk, sir, on the —?

MANAGER:
> Careful — don't step in the blood.

ASSISTANT: *Gently.*
> Are you feeling all right, sir?

MANAGER:
> Who. Who. Who.

THE LIGHTS SLOWLY FADE OUT.

THE PILE

a comedy in one act

Persons in the play:
        X, a businessman
        Y, an engineer

"The Pile" was first produced in 1970, in a version for radio, by the Canadian Broadcasting Corporation, in the series "CBC Tuesday Night." X was played by Mavor Moore and Y by Tommy Tweed. The program was produced and directed by Jean Bartels. It is included in the disc *Stories by Mavor Moore* distributed by CBC International.

The copying, either of separate parts or the whole of this work, by any process whatsoever, is forbidden by law and subject to the penalties prescribed in international law. All rights to produce "The Pile" in whole or in part, in any medium, are retained by the author. For information regarding permission and terms see copyright page.

A vacant lot, on the shore of a lake. Sounds of lapping water and the occasional cry of gulls come from the back of the theatre. Offstage an automobile drives up and stops. The door opens and shuts. X and Y come on slowly, down to the very front and centre of the stage; X carries a folding canvas stool and Y a seat-stick; X wears dirty construction shoes, Y wears galoshes. Both, as they approach down centre, seem to be scanning the audience — or scanning something which lies where the audience sits.

X:

Well, there it is.

Y:

Yes. There she is.

They survey, with a touch of possessive pride, what lies before them.

X:

Maybe we should say, there it lies.

Y:

No. *IS* is the word. It exists.

X:

You're existing if you just lie there.

Y:

That's not the point. If it was just lying there, hurting nobody, we wouldn't have to worry. It would be . . . passive. The fact that it exists, actively, is the problem.

X:

How . . . actively?

Y:

It'll begin to stink.

X:

I see what you mean.

Solemnly, each erects his sitting apparatus, and they sit — still contemplating what lies before them. A pause.

X: *Finally.*
What are we going to do about it?

Y:

You mean, what are we going to do *with* it.

X:

What's the difference?

Y:

You could leave it right there and still do something about it . . . like walking away.

X:

Well, why don't we?

Y:

Because we can't. It's ours. We have to do something *with* it. It's our responsibility. With it.

X:

I guess you're right.

A long stare out front, increasingly glum.

X:

What?

Y:

I didn't say anything.

X:

I mean, what do we do with it?

Y:

That's the problem.

X:

Then *what*?

Y:

Hmmm.

X:

Why don't we just . . . get rid of it?

Y:

How?

X:

I don't know . . . dump it somewhere?

Y:

With what?

X:

A dump truck.

Y:

A dump truck wouldn't take it . . . all that.

X:

Several loads? Back and forth, back and forth?

Y:

Back and forth! How would you get it in, in the first place?

X:

There must be some way.

Y:

As the fat lady said to the midget.   *Pause.*   Where would you put it?

X:

I don't know. The lake?

Y:

Can you imagine that in the lake? With all this talk about pollution?

X:

Nobody'd see us.

Y:

They'd soon find out. How long do you think you could keep a thing like that secret? They're always digging, dragging, analysing . . .

X: *Rising and going to look at the pile from a different angle.*
Well . . . you come up with something better, then.

Y:

I will if you'll let me think.

He thinks, silently: comes up with an idea, and discards it. Then he thoughtfully fills and lights his pipe.

X:

I wish we'd never done it. *He paces.*

Y:

Spilt milk.

X:

I wish we'd never got into the whole damn business.

Y:

It seemed like a good idea at the time.

X:

It wasn't my idea.

Y:

I wondered when that was going to come up.

X:

Well it wasn't.

Y:

What's that got to do with anything?

X:

Well, I mean you were the one who —

Y:

You went along with it. You thought it was a great idea. Terrific, you said. Colossal. A stroke of genius. I planted the seed; you grew it. Instead of implying it's all my fault, you should be grateful.

X:

All my life, I've wanted something we could do together. Your scientific knowledge, and my business know-how. Think of it, I used to say to myself: his scientific knowledge, and my business know-how.

Y:

Well, we got your scientific knowledge and *my* business know-how. Think of *that*.

X:

I am. I am, I am, I am.   *He sits again.*

Y:

Now we're stuck with it.

X:

Yes.   *He extracts a cigar, unwraps it and lights it.*

          Y rises, folds his seat back into a stick, and strides back and forth with it.

X:

Speaking of science . . .

Y:

I wasn't. You were.   *Continues pacing.*

X:

Well, what I mean is, isn't there some way we could just . . . make it vanish?

Y:

That's not science, that's magic.   *Lifting his stick.*   If this were a wand I'd have waved it long ago.

X:

I meant disintegrate it . . . scientifically. Like . . . well, burn it.

Y:

You think I haven't thought of that?

X:

I'm not a mind reader. You never mentioned it.

Y:

It won't burn.

X:

Pour kerosene over it.

Y:

It still wouldn't burn.

X:

You mean it's inflammable?

Y:

Inflammable means it *would* burn.

X:

No it doesn't — that's flammable.

Y:

There's no such word. Inflammable means what you think flammable means: you can in-flame it, ignite it, burn it up.

X:

You sure about that?

Y:

Allow me to know my business. Look it up if you want.

X: *Aggressively.*
All right then: is it *non*-inflammable?

Y:

That's what I said.

X:

That's not what you said. You said it wouldn't burn.

Y:

That's clear enough, for God's sake! — or would be to anyone less thick-headed.

X:

People in glass houses, et cetera. How am I supposed to know whether you mean that in its present state it isn't likely to catch fire — because it's too wet, or too gooey, or not gooey enough, or too hard, or too something — or that it literally can't be burnt up in whatever state it eventually gets to? Right? How am I supposed to know?

Y:

Because I tell you. Nothing whatever will make that stuff burn — short of a holocaust. Now have we got that straight?

X:

Don't snap at me — I'm only asking . . .

Y:

And I've told you!

X:

I haven't asked you yet.

Y:

Haven't asked me what?

X:

Whether it could be used for non-inflammability — you know, instead of asbestos, or whatever.

Y:

Christ. No.

X:

Why not?

Y:

Because you'd never — you can't cut it up; you can't fit it into places; you can't — well, it's not the right kind of material. It just isn't. The fact that it won't burn doesn't make it a candidate for anything special. There are lots of things you can't burn in the ordinary way. They're no special use to anybody. The point about asbestos is that you can *do* things with it. You can't do anything with *that*.

X:

I've thought of something else.

Y:

What?

X:

There isn't enough of it.

Y:

Well, that's another thing.

X:

I suppose we could always get more.

Y:

Not on your life. We've enough trouble now getting rid of this lot.

X:

Yes, that's the problem: getting rid of this.

Y:

Precisely.

Emphatically, he opens the top of the seat-stick and props himself on it.

X:

What about . . . couldn't we disintegrate it?

Y:

With what?

X:

Well, acid.

Y:

Honestly. That's only another form of burning.

X:

I thought it was eating. Acid is eating. Eating isn't burning.

Y:

I wish to god you'd leave the chemistry to people who know something about it.

X:

All right — but isn't there some way of . . . breaking it down? I mean, *you* tell *me*. Won't acid do that?

Y:

I really don't know where you get these fairy stories. If you could put it bit by bit in an acid bath for several days, you might. And how would we do that? We haven't got an acid bath, and even if we had we couldn't get it there to wherever the bath is that we haven't got. Right out here in the open, all of it, not a chance. So forget it.

X:

I was just trying to help.

Y:

Forget it.   *His pipe has gone out: he lights it.*

X now has a deep thought, and rises to frame it, eventually, into words.

X:

When I was a boy, I used to build puppet theatres. You wouldn't think there was much money in puppet theatres, would you?

Y:

No.

X:

There was then, for a kid. I got this commission to build a puppet theatre for a rich girl. They wanted to give it to her as a Christmas present, to go in the playroom, in the basement. They wanted all the trimmings, lights, curtains, everything. I made a beautiful theatre, spent all November and December on it, even with school and everything. It was to be a surprise. I got my older brother to rent a truck and we took it up there on Christmas Eve, up to their mansion in the suburbs. We couldn't get it in.

Y:

How do you mean, you couldn't get it in?

X:

It wouldn't go. It was too big. We couldn't get it through the front door, or the back door, or even the basement window.

Y:

What the hell has this got to do with anything?

X:

They wanted us to saw it in half. But if we'd sawed it in half that would have ruined the curtain tracks and the lighting circuits and a lot of other things.   *Pause.*   They wouldn't take it.   *Pause.*   Have you ever wondered what to do with a five-by-eight-foot puppet theatre nobody wanted?

Y:

Can't say I have.

X:

Well . . . I took it apart again, piece by piece, and used the pieces on something else. Disintegrated it. That's all I was asking.   *He sits again. His cigar has gone out: he relights it.*

They look at the pile, then at each other, then away.

Y:

I didn't say you couldn't break it up and use some of it.

X:

Yes you did.

Y:

I did not. You asked about making it vanish.

X:

Breaking it down.

Y:

Down is not up.

X:

What's the difference?

Y:

You break something down and you separate it into its constituent parts. You break something up and you get accidental pieces, like shattered glass.

X:

Well . . . if we could break down —

Y:

I'm not saying we could and I'm not saying we couldn't.

X:

But you said we could! That was the whole idea in the first

place . . . that if we went into this, we could make something of it, and get rid of it. That was the whole idea.

Y:

I said it was a reasonable risk. That's all I said. I said IF we could make something of it, and IF you could get rid of it, it represented a reasonable risk.

X:

How can I get rid of it unless you figure out something to get rid of in the first place?

Y:

What's the use of my figuring out something unless you've already figured out a way of getting rid of it after? Try to be logical.

X:

I am trying.

Y:

The problem is basically logistical.

X:

I'm *trying* to be logical.

Y:

I said logistical. Logistics has nothing to do with logic.

X:

But you said —

Y:

Logistics has to do with lodging. Finding lodgings for . . . whatever it is. This is a problem in distribution, and that's not my specialty, it's yours. Now: there she is. Never mind your crying over spilt milk, never mind your recriminations — the question is, purely and simply, how do we get rid of it. And that, my friend, is *your* responsibility.

X:

Yes.

Y rises: moves closer to the pile, examining it.

Y:

Why couldn't you palm it off on a contractor?

X:

What for?   *Rising to join Y: peering closely.*

Y:

Don't they need something . . . just to fill things with?

X:

Not just anything. You can't fill things up with just anything.

Y:

Then *what?*

X:

Well, if you could grind it down, make material that would set . . .

Y:

Dumping it back in *my* lap, are you?

X:

Well . . . I mean, I don't know what you'd come up with. So how can I tell whether a contractor would need it?

Y:

If you just *give* it to him — give it to him if he'll only come and take it away. Then let him figure out what to make of it.

X:

Why would he go to all the trouble and expense of carrying it away unless he wanted it for something?

Y:

Can't you think of something he would want it for?

X:

No.

Y:

There you are, you see. Negative thinking. *X is about to reply, but thinks better of it and walks away. Y is thinking furiously.*

X:

I suppose it's ridiculous to ask, but what about fertilizer?

Y:

What about it?

X:

I was wondering about the farmers. I mean I could flog it to farmers if you could think of a way to make it into fertilizer.

Y:

It's a thought.

X:

You mean we — it could . . .

Y:

Not really.

X:

But is it possible?

Y:

Possible but not probable.

X:

But if there's a possibility . . . .

Y:

Theoretically possible, but practically impossible.

X:

But you said —

Y:

How would you handle it? What process? What equipment? And what would you have when you were finished?

X:

Shit.

Y:

Like drinking a double martini to get the olive pit. A waste of time and effort.   *He walks away.*

X:

No good, eh?

Y:

No.

Leaving X to think furiously, Y goes to the extreme right, and then to extreme left, studying the pile from the sides.

Y:

I'm wondering . . .

X:

About breaking it down?

Y:

About breaking it up.

X:

Into what?

Y:

Toys.

X:

Toys?!

Y:

They make toys out of amazing things these days: sticks, stones, shells, rags, nuts, berries . . .

X:

Be serious. You think we're playing games?

Y:

    Games can be bloody serious. Now put your mind to it: couldn't one *play* with it . . . somehow?

X:

    For fun?

Y:

    Of course.

X:

    I don't see how, looking at it.

Y:

    Use your imagination.

X:

    I am.

Y:

    Take a good look.

X: *Having done so, from several angles.*
    You mean, paint it up? . . . red, yellow, blue — that sort of thing?

Y:

    Little pieces of it. Toys are little.

X:

    Some toys are big. If you made a park around it and painted the whole thing bright red —

Y:

    I'm not talking about painting the whole thing.

X:

    How would you break it up, then?

Y:

    Trying to put it onto me again, eh!

X:

I just want to know how you'd break it up.

Y:

It's just a hypothesis. IF we could break it up . . .

X:

Well, IF we could break it up, what about sculpture?

Y:

What about it?

X:

You've seen what they use these days: scrap metal, chunks of this and that, old chairs, pieces of anything. They come and pick it up, carry it off, weld it all together and sell it for a mint.

Y:

I don't exactly know how you'd weld *that*.

X:

But if you could break it up, you could put it together again.

Y:

That doesn't follow at all. Half the things in the world, you smash them up and that's that. Humpty-Dumpty. Besides, how many sculptors are there anyway? Put them all in one room and you couldn't have a party.

X:

They might take *some* of it.

Y:

Then what do we do with the rest of it?

X:

I hadn't thought of that.

Y:

Hmph.   *He opens his stick and sits again.*

Sadly shaking his head, X sits and picks dirt off his shoes.

X:

In all my life, I never thought I'd have to handle a thing like this. Where did we go wrong?

Y:

You expect justice in this life?

X:

No. But there's no escaping judgement. I've worked hard, I've tried to do the right thing . . . and now to have it end like this.

Y:

This isn't the end.

X:

We'll never get out of this one. This one's done it.

Y:

Never say die until you're dead.

X:

It's that sort of silly optimism that got us into this.

Y:

Now you're blaming me again.

X:

I'm not blaming you. I'm to blame.

Y:

I never said that.

X:

I'm saying it. I've had it coming. It's all very well for you, working away in your lab or wherever, sitting up in your ivory tower . . . but you don't get far in business without cutting a few corners now and then. I've got away with a good deal, so far. Now it's caught up with me. It's as if that . . . out there . . . is what I've been piling up all my life . . . a little bit here and a little bit there . . . until it's got too big to ignore.

94

Too big to get rid of. And even if you could, *how* could you? Where do you hide it? You can't even break it up and do something with the pieces. We're stuck with it. There it is, starting to stink, not just lying there — you're right — swelling out of its own rot . . . indisposable. We're the disposables.

Y:

We're not disposed of yet.   *He rises, walks about with the stick.*

X:

It's what we deserve.

Y:

Speak for yourself. How do you know what we deserve?

X:

It's a judgement.

Y:

It's nothing of the kind. Superstitious nonsense, that's what it is. Next you'll be telling me it's an Act of God, who arranged the way you part your hair, or would if he'd seen fit to leave you any . . . that there is providence in the fall of a sparrow, let alone yours truly, and that we'd better like it or lump it. Well, I don't like it and I don't propose to lump it, God or no God.

X:

It wouldn't hurt to pray.

Y:

It wouldn't help to pray — unless grovelling gives you some sort of lift. We got ourselves into this, and we'll get ourselves out of it.

X:

How?

Y:

I'll think of a way if you'll stop drivelling about judgement and give me a chance to think.

95

X:

Go ahead. God helps those who help themselves.

Y:

And they're precisely the ones who don't need his help. Now shut up.

X:

All right . . . but I can think too, can't I?

Y:

If you can refrain from passing judgement long enough.

X:

We'll both think. Hard.

Y:

Right.   *He pauses, leaning on the stick in front of him.*

They both think furiously. X takes out a notebook, consults it, shakes his head and returns it to his pocket.

X:

Have you thought of anything yet?

Y:

I'm getting there.

X rises and paces.

Y:

You can't think of any single thing it could be flogged for?

X:

No.

Y:

And you can't think of any single thing it could be given away for, if only someone would come and take it away?

X:

No. Unless . . .   *Stops.*

Y:

What?

X:

Lamely.
Unless you can think of something useful that could be made
out of it. Can you think of anything useful that could be made
out of it? Or from it? Or with it?

Y:

A glint in his eye.
What you mean is, is there a way of breaking it up . . . or
down . . . so that what's left over might be put to some useful
purpose for someone?

X:

If you like.

Y:

Well, I can't think of one.

X:

Aggressively.
That's the first time you've said that. Earlier you said perhaps.
You said you couldn't say yes and you wouldn't say no.

Y:

I did not. That was only about breaking it down or up. I didn't
say anything whatever about distributing the residue as a useful
product. That's not my department, it's yours.

X:

All right, then: can it be broken up or down?

Y:

Possibly. In the long run, of course, everything disintegrates.
The whole world is disintegrating — a process known as entropy.
In the long run it's neither here nor there whether it's here or
there.

X:

Never mind the long run. What about the short run? What do
we do today so it'll be gone tomorrow?

Y:

Can't you see I'm trying to come at it scientifically, by a process of elimination?

X:

We've eliminated everything except the thing we're trying to eliminate.

Y:

No we haven't. Not yet. We've got bogged down in a chicken or egg conundrum, whether we start with how to get rid of something, or with the something you get rid of. The real problem, if we may please avoid these irrelevant philosophical blind alleys, is that it exists, as such, and a way must be found of putting an end to its existence. It is, and it must not be.

X:

Where do we go from there?

Y:

We must eliminate the positives before we examine the negative. If there is no earthly use to which it can be put, then — and only then — should we look at the alternative.

X:

Right.

Y:

Now then.   *Indicating the pile.*   It becomes apparent that it cannot be burnt up, broken up, sold up, or even given up. It's a question of it or us.

X:

You forgot one up.

Y:

Pardon?

X:

You left out one kind of up.

Y:

What are you talking about?

X:

You never mentioned blowing up.

Y:

What: you mean with dynamite, or something?

X:

Why not? We could drill a hole down the middle, way down into the ground, drop in a stick of dynamite, and blow it up.

Y:

That would make a worse mess than we've got now.

X:

How would it be worse?

Y:

Some of it would be under, but some of it would be on top.

X:

It would depend.

Y:

That's not the main problem, anyway. You haven't even thought of the main problem.

X:

What?

Y:

We don't own the land. We only rented it. You can't blow up property you don't own.

X:

We own what's on it.

Y:

That's not the point.

X: *Turning away.*
Well, you come up with something better, then.

Y:

Just let me think, that's all.   *He makes the seat, and sits where*
he is.

          X sits, coolly: the responsibility has been lifted from his shoulders.

Y:

When I was at college, we did an experiment . . . with plastic.
We were supposed to fill a few molds with the stuff. We had all
the makings there for the whole class, which was quite a lot. The
mix went into a large tube which fed into the molds, and you
shut it off after each fill. Well, the spigot stuck and we couldn't
turn the damn thing off. It overflowed all the molds, the tables,
the equipment, everything . . . and set. Not a thing we could
do except break everything off and throw it out. Nothing you
could do with the plastic. Not a thing.   *He rises and walks*
away.

X: *After a bemused pause; expecting more to have followed.*
What was the point of all that?

Y:

I'm thinking it through. A hypothesis.

X:

Thinking what through? What hypothesis?

Y:

At least it's more to the point than you and your puppet theatre.

X:

That was just . . . a parable.

Y:

So is this. You were stuck with it, so you broke it up. You
couldn't very well break up the house it was supposed to go into.

X:

Hardly.

Y:

We've been concentrating on the contents instead of the container — don't you see? There are two ways of getting rid of anything: throw away the contents, or throw away the container.

X:

I'm trying to follow you . . .   *Rises, joins Y.*

Y:

We've got to forget about that, out there, and put our minds to what contains it.

X:

Contains it?

Y:

The land — don't you see? The moment you brought up the land it's sitting on, I should have got it.

X:

But you said we couldn't. You said —

Y:

I said we couldn't leave it in a mess. But if we did it neatly . . .

X:

I wish you'd just tell me.

Y:

I'm wondering . . .

X:

Yes . . .

Y:

I'm wondering if there isn't some way to bury it.

X:

Bury it where?

Y:

Right here.

X:

Just dig a hole and bury it?

Y:

Yes.

X:

It would have to be a big hole.

Y:

Well?

X:

And you said it wasn't our property.

Y:

Well?

X:

An awful lot of digging.

Y:

What would that matter? We're not burying treasure, we wouldn't want it back again. Once it's dug, the hole wouldn't be ours, it would be his.

X:

No. The hole would still be ours.   *Searching for a document in all his pockets.*   If he didn't like it he could insist we take the hole away.

Y:

How can you take away a hole? It's what's in it that matters.

X:

But you said to forget the contents and concentrate on the container. The container would be the hole.

Y:

No! The land would be the container.

X: *He finds the document.*
But the land isn't ours . . . it says so right here!

Y:

Look! We dig a hole, put it in, put the earth back on top, and leave the land just as it was — it's as simple as that! Why worry about the hole?

X:

Because you can't just dig a hole and leave it there on someone else's property!

Y:

You're not just digging a hole, you're filling it up!

X:

Yes, but look what you're filling it with, and it isn't even your hole!

Y:

You said it was! That was the whole point of your objection: that the hole would still be ours. Now you say it would be his.

X: *Searching through the document.*
I meant the land that was making the hole would still be his. We'd be making our hole on someone else's property, and he'd have a perfect right to come along and tell us to take OUR hole off HIS land. I'll find it — I'll show you.

Y:

Once and for all, it's not the hole, it's what's in it.

X:

— Including what's in it.

Y:

How do you mean, including!

X:

He'd have a perfect right to come along and tell us to take the hole and what's in it off his land.

Y: *Sighing.*
Not if it's buried. Not if it's down under.

X:

Why not?

Y:

What does he care what's underneath?

X: *Pointing to the clause he has finally found.*
He owns the mineral rights.

Y:

Why in the name of God bring that up!

X:

Because it's here in the lease.

Y:

But the stuff is worthless! We've already established that. What we'd bury there is absolutely worthless. It's no good to us — what good would it be to him?

X:

That's not the point. He'd have mineral rights over something that's ours.

Y:

But we don't want it!

X:

Then why would he want it?

Y:

He wouldn't want it. He'd be stuck with it.

X slowly takes this in: looks at the document again, and then nods in worry. The light thickens.

X:

That . . . wouldn't be fair.

Y:

I didn't say it would be. We took a risk, he took a risk when he rented the land to us to put it on. Even-stephen.

X:

It wouldn't be right. It's only a six-month lease.

Y:

With an option.

X:

That doesn't change anything. When he comes along and finds out what we've buried here . . .

X shakes his head and puts the document back in his pocket.

Y:

Maybe he'd never find out. Maybe he'd use it for something that didn't need digging.

X:

But what if he did find out?

Y:

Maybe he'd be able to figure out some way of using it . . .

X:

We couldn't.

Y:

Still, *he* might.

Y knocks the ash out of his pipe. X comes over with a gleam in his eye and nudges Y.

X:

Then . . . why bury it?

Y:

What?

X:

I mean, if he could figure out a way of using it . . .

Y:

He might.

X:

Or if he could figure out a way of getting rid of it . . .

Y:

He might.

X:

. . . why not leave it right out there in the open! We wouldn't need to go to all the trouble of burying it, and he wouldn't need to go to all the trouble of digging it up again.

Y:

Hmmm.

X:

And another thing. If he couldn't figure out a way of using it . . .

Y:

We couldn't . . .

X:

. . . And if he couldn't figure out a way of getting rid of it . . .

Y:

We couldn't . . .

X:

. . . Then what could he do but bury it?

Y:

And if HE buried it, on his own land . . .

X:

Then the hole wouldn't be ours . . . it would be his.

Y:

And then . . . he'd be . . . stuck . . . with it.

X:

Yes.

> *Slowly, they both fold up their seats, and look again, fondly, at the pile.*

Y:

I guess that's the solution.

X:

Just to leave it. Walk away, and leave it.

Y:

Not do anything.

X:

After all, it isn't really our responsibility.

Y:

That's right. I mean, there it is.

X:

Yes — there she is.

> *They take a last look out over their erstwhile property.*

Y:

Let's go.

> *They drift off, turning to look back as they go.*
> *FADE-OUT.*

GETTING IN

an interview in one act

Persons in the play:
P., an official
T., an applicant

An early version of ''Getting In'' was heard on both CBC Radio and
BBC Radio in 1969, and in the same year a stage version was published
by Samuel French, New York. Its first appearances as a television play,
in both Canada and Britain, were in 1971. The CBC-TV production,
in the series ''Program X,'' was directed by Herb Roland, with Colin
Fox as the Official and Gerard Parkes as the Applicant. The BBC-
TV production, in the series ''Thirty Minute Theatre,'' was produced
by Anne Head and directed by John Hefin, with Robert Hardy as
the Official and Joss Ackland as the Applicant.

The time is today, the place a front office. There is a large desk with a chair behind it, and another chair facing it. A coat-tree stands near the entrance. Since the establishment concerned must not be identifiable, the less additional scenery the better; but other furnishings found in almost any office, such as a filing cabinet and lighting fixture, may be used sparingly. If a box set is used, its design should be as vague and ambiguous as possible, and there should under no circumstances be a window.

The official, P., whose job is to interview all applicants to the establishment, is middle-aged, correct and well dressed. The applicant, T., about the same age, has made an effort to dress in his most acceptable jacket and slacks.

P: *Leading the way as they enter.*
Come in, Mr. Thomas. Let me take your coat.

T: *Following.*
Thank you.

P: *As he hangs up T.'s coat and hat.*
Come in and sit down.

T:

Thanks.   *Sits, looks about.*

P:

You like our place?

T:

Yes.   *Laughs.*   So far, anyway.

P: *If there is a door he closes it: crosses to desk.*
Good. We think you'll like it here.

T:

What I've seen so far is . . . um . . .

P:

You'd like it.

T:

It's very nice.

P: *After making himself comfortable in the desk chair.*
It is what you expected?

T:

Pretty well. When I heard —

P:

Of course you haven't met the others, yet.

T:

That's right.   *Confidently:*   But so far everything's . . . you know . . .

P:

Good.   *Taking a clipboard from the side drawer.*   We hope
it's what you've been looking for.

T:

Oh yes, I'm sure.

P: *Extracting a document from a file in the same drawer.*
We have your application here, of course, and your curriculum
vitae . . .

T:

Was it what you wanted?

P: *Arranging papers.*
Fine, as far as it goes. May I ask you to fill me in on a few things?

T:

Naturally. I expected . . . well . . .

P: *Looking at him blandly first.*
What did you expect?

T:

Well, I mean, I imagined there'd be a few . . . you know, formalities.

P:

Attaching the document to the clipboard — which he holds throughout. Nothing to worry about, Mr. Thomas. We just want to make sure you'll be happy here.   *Takes pencil from desk set.*

T:

Oh, I *know!*

P:

Glancing at document.
It's a big step you're taking.

T:

Well, yes! I didn't exactly mean formalities. I meant, you know, getting into a place like this, you have to —

P:

But you don't mind?

T:

Hell, no! I mean there's nothing, um . . . well, you know what you want to ask, what you have to know. So fire ahead.

P:

It's just that in addition to the bare facts, we like to have —

T: *Genially.*
It's quite all right, honestly!

P:

And after all you've been through to get here . . .

T: *He looks at P. in fear, then looks bleakly away.*
Everything's . . . all right now.

P: *Cheerfully.*
Right. Now you list yourself as 'separated.'

T:

That's right. Not divorced, just . . . separated.

P: *Making a note, as he continues to do throughout.*
Let me ask you: what's your attitude toward children?

T:

The kids? Well, you know, I miss them a good deal, especially —

P:

Not your own. I mean children in general. Do you find them, for example, a nuisance?

T:

They can be. It's good to get away from them.

P:

But you'd miss them?

T: *Thinking first.*
No. May I smoke?   *He searches through his pockets, fruitlessly.*

P:

Certainly.   *He produces an ashtray.*   Of course, without contact with young people you might cut yourself off from the future, don't you think?

T: *Rising, he crosses to the coat-tree and finds his cigarettes and lighter in his raincoat, talking as he does so.*
Well — huh! — I'm not mad about the future, the way things are going. Kids these days — drugs, violence. That's one reason I want to get in here.

P:

Are you afraid of the future? You feel threatened by it?

T:

Not exactly.   *He sits again.*   I'm not looking for a, you know, a refuge or anything. It's just, how can you tell what's going to happen next? Someday someone'll push a button, and . . .
He lights his cigarette. After this he more or less chain-smokes.

114

P:

You're not afraid of what might happen to you *here?*

T:

Oh, no. I mean if I was with others who . . .   *Shrugs.*
I've never felt I really belonged, you know what I mean? Not
today. These times.

P:

Would you have preferred to live in some other time?

T:

Well, I mean, when you knew where you stood. Like, when
society had values . . . when you could believe in decency and
morality . . . when people knew the difference between right and
wrong, and when you saw a thing was right you did it. You see,
that's what I like about the idea of a place like this. It's kind
of a, you know, oasis.

P:

Not a refuge.

T:

No, no. Someplace to recharge your batteries, more like that.
Look, I really don't care about kids, one way or the other. I mean
I can get along without them.   *As P. hesitates:*   You
can put that down.

P: *Doing so.*
And women?

T:

What about them?

P:

Can you get along without them?

T:

Don't you allow women?

P:

The question is not so much what we allow, Mr. Thomas, as what you were expecting. A question of attitude.

T:

You mean am I gay, or something? I like women . . .

P:

Ah. How much?

T:

Well, I'm not, you know, perfect. If you have to 've lived like a monk . . .

P:

It's not a matter of how you have lived, but of how you're prepared to live.

T: *Joking.*
You want me to live like a monk?

P:

I want to see what you're prepared to do, Mr. Thomas, if we take you in. Would you object, for example, to obeying certain orders in regard to your sexual life?

T:

Well, I mean, it would depend.

P:

Depend on what?

T:

On what the orders were.

P:

Not on you, I take it.

T:

Well, I'd go along with any *reasonable* restrictions . . .

P:

I don't believe I referred to restrictions. The point is not what you wouldn't do but what you would — if you were asked to.

T:

Look, I've been around, but I've never done . . . I mean, there's plenty I haven't done, things I've read about . . . and how do I know —

P:

Please, Mr. Thomas, I'm only trying to find out what you had in mind. Your past interests us only insofar as it may affect your future. Our future. We *want* you to join us, but it would be unfair to you to let you in, only for you to find out too late that you didn't belong.

T:

Yes. Yes, I see that.

P:

Right.   *He turns to the next page of the document.*   Now, we've reviewed your financial statement.

T:

It's okay, isn't it?

P:

So far as it goes, fine.

T:

I mean, the entrance fee is there — certified cheque the way you wanted.

P:

Yes.

T:

And my credit is good.

P:

Neither solvency nor credit is quite apposite, Mr. Thomas. We have no means test here.

T:

Then what? I mean, what more do you need?

P:

We're interested in your business experience.   *He rises, sits on the desk.*   You've held a good many different jobs . . .

T:

Oh, yes! Lots of experience, if that's what you want.

P:

But you don't seem to have stayed in them very long.

T:

Well, you know, I like variety. I've had good luck and bad.

P:

So I see.

T: *A double take.*
Oh, you mean that time. Well, you can't win 'em all. I got in pretty deep that time.

P:

Deep into what?

T: *Shifting in his chair.*
Well, it was . . . everything piled up, and I . . . I had to take a chance I wouldn't ordinarily have taken.

P:

You gambled?

T:

Not on horses, or games, or anything like that. I wouldn't like you to get the wrong idea. It was a, you know, a business venture. I had bad luck. My partners. They took me. You know.

P:

And the other times?

T:

What other times?

P:

The times you had good luck.

T: *Serious, defensive.*
I earned every cent, the hard way.

P: *Rises, walks U. L.*
And what would you expect to bring us, if you came in?

T:

Well, all my experience.

P: *Turning back to him.*
What experience have you had at business techniques like
larceny, extortion, bribery . . . ?

T: *Momentarily stopped.*
I don't think I . . . you mean I have to 've . . .

P: *Standing, L. of desk.*
I'm only trying to discover what it is you want to find here. What:
honesty? corruption? justice? What?

T:

Now look.   *He rises and leans across the desk.*   I've had
to cut a few corners in my time, but if you're looking for
sharpies . . . I mean, I can cut corners as well as the next man
— but I thought if I got in here —

P: *Coolly.*
Mr. Thomas, you get rather easily bored, don't you?

T:

What?

P:

You bore easily. A man who has held so many jobs, who is always
looking for something new . . .

T:

Oh, I see what you mean. Yes, I guess I do.   *Sits back
confidently.*   It takes something really worthwhile to hold me.
Something stimulating. Yes.

P:

When you get bored, do you wish you could just take off and
do exciting things?   *Crosses behind T.*

T:

Doesn't everybody?

P:

What exciting things?

T:

Well, you know . . .

P:

I'm asking you. What excites you?

T:

I like to have fun.

P:

Is that what you expect to find here?

T:

Well, yes!

P:

What kind of fun?

T:

Well, not always just *fun,* maybe — I mean I know it's serious,
or I wouldn't be trying to get in — but you have to have fun
sometimes.

P:

Yes, but what is fun to you? A film? A riot? A dance? A
striptease? Pub-crawling? Poker? What?

T:

Now wait a minute —!

P:

I'm trying to find out what excites you.

T:

Lots of things, but not — I mean, I'll go along with the game!
Where ever *you* find *your* fun is fine with me!

P: *From behind T., quietly.*
Mr. Thomas, have you ever used a pistol?   *No response.*
Have you?

T: *Eventually.*
Not . . . for a long time.

P:

Have you ever killed a man?

T: *Eventually.*
Not since the war. Do you have to put that down?

P:

Would you be prepared to kill again?

T:

I don't know. But I certainly didn't expect —

P:

Of course you didn't.   *He sits in his own chair.*   I'm
beginning to wonder, Mr. Thomas, whether you'll do. We

have a long waiting list, and we —

T:

Why? What have I said?

P:

All this defensiveness. All this . . . indirection. Will you fit in here, I ask myself.

T:

Look, I'm doing my best to answer your questions. But some of the things you're asking me . . . I never thought it would be like this!   *He rises and paces.*   If I have to be that kind of person to get in —

P:

What kind of person?

T:

I've been pretty adaptable. I haven't said no. I haven't just said I wouldn't. I've tried to go along.

P:

Go along with what?

T:

With what you people do here. And some of it —

P:

But, Mr. Thomas, I haven't told you what we do here.

T:

Well, you've implied —

P:

Oh, no. You have inferred. I have been asking the simplest of questions, very *direct* questions, to find out whether you will fit in. We have other people to consider.

T:

I know that.

P:

And of course you do want to belong.

T:

That's why I'm here.

P:

All right.

T: *Coming to desk, leaning on it.*
But you said . . . you were wondering, you said.

P:

If you'd fit in. I felt I had to be frank.

T:

You mean I won't?

P:

Well . . . let's see. Please sit down.   *Turning to the next page as T. sits.*   Let's go on. Mr. Thomas, how do you regard tidiness?

T:

Oh, I'm very tidy.   *A little late, he crosses his legs and primps his clothes.*

P:

I mean in others. Do you like other people to be tidy?

T:

Of course.

P:

And what would you do if they were not tidy?

T:

Oh, well!

P:

No, tell me.

T:

Well, I'd . . . I'd . . . try to get them to tidy up.

P:

And if they didn't?

T:

Well, you'd just have to get rid of them.

P:

How?

T: *Lighting another cigarette.*
I don't know. How *do* you get rid of people here? Expel them?

P:

Would you punish them?

T:

Sure. Punish them.

P:

How? Solitary confinement?

T:

If you like.

P:

Hard labour?

T:

Why not?!

P:

Whipping?

T:

Well, I mean, if it's serious.

P:

Capital punishment?   *He rises and circles T.*

How serious is untidiness, Mr. Thomas?

T: *Hedging: nervous at the note-taking.*
It can get very serious. I mean . . . rats and disease.

P: Pollution?

T: Well, that's certainly a kind of untidiness. People shouldn't be allowed to pollute a place. It's terrible what we're doing to our, you know, environment.

P: And what about mental pollution?

T: How do you mean?

P: People who are untidy in their minds, and go around messing up other people's ideas.

T: I don't know. I never thought of that kind of pollution.

P: And would you also punish those who are mentally untidy and destructive?

T: Sure. I mean you've got to have some order around the place. And if people . . . well, if some people didn't fit in, then . . .

P: *Now* you're beginning to grasp it, Mr. Thomas! Well done! *Sits in his own chair.* Now what about sharing?

T: Sharing?

P:

Do you mind sharing with others?

T:

Certainly not! I'm for share and share alike.

P:

Splendid.

T:

Sharing what?

P:

Well . . . let's say your living quarters, your worldly goods, your spirit.

T:

Can I take those one at a time?

P:

Of course.

T: *Making himself comfortable.*
By living quarters, do you mean just . . . separate but equal? or living all together with no place of your own?

P:

It's a problem, isn't it! Do I get the impression you'd prefer to have a place of your own?

T:

Others could come there.

P:

On your terms?

T:

Well, if it was mine. All I need's a corner — I'm not asking for anything grand.

P:

And your worldly goods?

T:

I haven't all that much to share.

P:

That is the test.

T:

If I had more I'd be glad to share it.

P:

Then it would be no test.

T:

Why wouldn't it?

P:

The test is precisely that: to share what you cannot afford to part with.

T:

Oh, I see what you mean. Well, when you put it like that, I mean, you can have . . . you know, anything that's mine is yours.

P:

Anything?

T: *Eventually.*
   I'd need to keep a few things.

P:

What, for instance?

T:

Well, you know . . . my things. My clothes, a few pieces of furniture, a few books, my glasses, a couple of pictures . . . things like that. They wouldn't be much use to anybody else.

127

P:

How do you know?

T:

Well, they're personal.

P:

That's the whole point, Mr. Thomas. Would you be willing to part, say, with your passport? Your driver's license? Your identification card?

T: *Rising, almost attacking P.*
Now look: if getting into this place . . . if you're just sounding me out on my, you know, philosophy, that's one thing. But if you're expecting me to give up *everything* — if you have rules like that —

P: *Calmly.*
Don't imagine for a moment that I'm making — or applying — gratuitous rules. But we have to be sure you'll fit in, *of your own free will.* Please do sit down. Now how about your spirit?

T: *Sitting, troubled.*
I don't think I know what you mean.

P:

Perhaps the word is old fashioned. Let me put it this way: when you are happy, do you like to share that happiness with others?

T:

Oh, yes. Naturally.

P:

And when others are depressed, would you share their depression?

T:

If . . . anyone wants to come and talk to me . . . you know, bend my ear . . .

P:

If *they* come and seek you out.

T:

Well, yes. How else would you know?

P:

Let us change the subject.　　　　*Turns to next page.*　　　　You
have lived in various places.

T:

Yes, I have.

P:

Do you enjoy meeting people who are . . . different?

T:

Different from what?

P:

From you. From each other.

T:

Well, up to a point.

P:

What point? Could you live among thieves?

T:

That's getting pretty different.

P:

Really? What about a slum in Rio de Janeiro?

T:　　　*Trying to make a joke of it.*
I don't know . . . I've never been there.

P:

Could you live on a diet of rotten rice . . . or raw fish?

T:

Well, if I had to. I mean, I know there are places where you have to, but why would I have to here?

P:

There are certain times and places that test us. Could you, for example, cut off your own leg?

T: *Sitting up uncomfortably.*
No.

P:

Why not?

T:

I don't know why not.

P:

Are you afraid?

T:

No, it's not that.

P:

Then what is it?

T:

I just . . . I just . . . don't like to touch my own body.

P:

Good! Now we're getting down to it.   *From the centre drawer, P. takes out a clinical flashlight and some attachable filters. He then reaches for a switch on the U. side of the desk and turns down the lights.*   Are you sensitive to colour?   *He attaches a red filter to the lens.*

T:

What colour?

P: *Switching on flashlight and turning it directly into T.'s eyes.*
Does red excite you?

T:

Sometimes. I don't know.

P:

What does the colour red mean to you?

T:

Well: fire, stop, anger, blood . . .

P:

Blood. Good.   *Without hurrying, he changes the filter: shines it at T.*   And blue?

T:

Blue?

P:

What does blue mean to you?

T:

I don't know . . . Cold, the sea, the sky . . .

P:

Anything else?

T:

Death.

P:

Ah.   *He unhurriedly turns off the flashlight, switches on the main light, removes the filter and replaces the flashlight; then makes a note.*

T:

Why . . . why do you want to know things like that?

P:

It all helps, Mr. Thomas, it all helps. Now then.   *Turns to the next page.*   You say here you are a Protestant.

T:

That's right. I mean, that's what I always put. But it doesn't mean much. You don't have religious discrimination, do you? Because I'm easy, I —

P:

We have all kinds of people here, but obviously, if you are to become one of us, there must be some common ground.

T:

Sure, sure.

P:

It would make no sense, for instance, to put together, in close proximity, head hunters and girl guides. Now then: what do you believe in?

T: *He thinks: then confidently.*
Well, I guess I believe in God.

P:

Which? Whose?

T:

Same one as everybody else. I mean, when you get right down to it, everybody has the same idea.

P:

What same idea?

T:

Well . . . you know, a mysterious force . . . whatever runs things.

P:

How?

T:

He just does. No mystery, otherwise.

P:

Are you afraid of God?

T:

In a way. I mean, He's got the upper hand.

P:

Then why does He allow things to go wrong?

T:

Maybe it all comes out in the wash. I mean, maybe it just looks
that way now, but all the time He knows what He's doing.

P: *Rising and circling T.*
Then you wouldn't object, say, if God were to punish you?

T:

No, I don't think so. I've done . . . well, I expect some
punishment. *He stubs his cigarette.*

P: *From T.'s right.*
And if his servants were to punish you, you wouldn't object?

T:

You mean here? Is *that* your idea? *Half rising to face*
him. Is that what I'm getting into?

P: *Tossing the clipboard onto the desk.*
You can always withdraw your application, Mr. Thomas.

T:

I didn't mean that. *Now rising fully and facing P.*
Look, I'm easy! — but don't get the idea I'm looking for punishment. I'm not exactly a, you know, masochist.

P:

I'm only trying to find out what you believe, Mr. Thomas. Do
you believe in the Devil?

T:

I don't *know!* I just go along like everybody else, doing my
best, one day at a time. But I'd like to believe in something.
Nobody does these days — and I'd like to get in somewhere
where people *do* know. So if you have some special belief, if you

133

want me to sign up and say I believe the same as you do . . . I mean, count me in!

P: *Crossing to sit in his own chair, then picking up the board again.* Then you believe in nothing?

T:

I wouldn't say that.   *He sits too.*   I believe in the Golden Rule — you know . . . Do as you would be done by, that sort of thing.

P:

Respect others as you respect yourself?

T:

Something like that.

P:

And do you respect yourself?

T:

Yes! . . . on the whole, yes.

P:

On the whole?

T: *His hands beginning to stray aimlessly.* Well, I mean, I've done things I don't respect myself for . . .

P:

Such as what?

T:

Do I have to go into everything?

P:

Mr. Thomas: are you a nervous man?

T:

No! I've told you, I don't like to touch myself.

P:

Then why do you?

T:

I'm not. I'm avoiding . . . touching myself.

P:

Are you ashamed of yourself, then?

T:

No.

P:

Of *something* about yourself? What is it you don't respect? What don't you like to touch?

T:

What's that got to do with anything, for God's sake!

P:

Mr. Thomas, what do you see when you look in that mirror?   *Indicating a mirror on the "fourth wall."*

T:

In the mirror?   *He slowly rises, moves down to look more closely.*

P:

What do you see? That's your own body, your own face. What do you see?

T:

I don't like my face, if that's what you mean.

P:

You don't?

T:

I'm not gone on myself, if that's what you're driving at. Wrinkles, bags. I mean, look at it. Mouth lopsided, nose too big. Eyes . . .

P:

What about the eyes?

T:　　　*Glancing at P. then back to the mirror.*
I don't like the way they look at me, if you want to know: always reproaching me . . .

P:

That's it, Mr. Thomas, that's it! What are your own eyes expecting of you?

T:　　　*Into the mirror.*
Nobody ever gave a damn. Who the hell cares? My father? My mother? Gave me a face but they didn't give a damn. Take it and run. You get me and I'll get you. Lay each other in the back of a car, world falling apart, who the hell cares? Add a litter to the litter. One more poor bastard. You get me and I'll get you. You can't call it my fault. I've looked after myself, I'm nobody's fool, I've made mistakes same as everyone else — but I know, God damn it I know, when I'm boxed in, beating my head against the bloody walls — I didn't make the box, but I know when I'm in it, when I've got to get out of the box — when my face, my hands, my legs, my balls — I've got to get out of my skin. *I've got to get out!*　　　*Turns to P.*　　　That's . . . why I've got to . . . get in. Don't you see? That's why I've got to get in here.　　　*Leaning over the desk.*　　　That's why you've got to take me! I've got to belong somewhere — and this . . . honest to God, it's the only place left.　　　*He sits, spent.*

P:　　　*Closing the document and removing it from the clipboard.*
We don't, Mr. Thomas, have to take anybody.

T:　　　*Pathetically.*
Please, I'll do anything you want, anything you say . . .

P:

Precisely.　　　*He puts the board away in the drawer, leaving the document out.*

T:

I know I said the wrong things —

P:

That is not the point . . .

T: *Slowly rising.*
I didn't know what it was you wanted me to say — and you were writing everything down . . .

P:

I quite understand.

T:

If only you'd told me what the rules were, what was expected of me . . .

P:

I did *explain.* I told you I was only trying to find out what you expected of us. There's no use your wanting to belong if you can't.

T: *Alternately moving away and turning on him.*
But I do! I didn't mean what I said about killing people. I'm against war!

P:

That's not good enough, Mr. Thomas.

T:

Then why didn't you ask me? I'll fight. Write *that* down.

P:

Please, Mr. Thomas —

T:

You've got me all wrong! I'm not *that* crazy about being tidy. I'll share, I'll share anything.

P:

Your living quarters, your worldly goods, your spirit?

T:

Those were your words, not mine. I don't know what the hell your arrangements are here! I'm willing to go along with anything reasonable — but I don't know what kind of answer you expected to questions like that.

P:

I know, I know.

T:

I can learn to get along anywhere. Haven't I been doing that all my life? I know I've made a mess of things so far — but I'm willing to make amends. I mean, look: whatever it is you want me to be or do, I'll be like that, I'll do it. You want to punish me, go right ahead. I deserve it.

P:

We don't want to punish you, Mr. Thomas.

T:

No, go right ahead!

P:

We wanted you to come in with us, we really did. We thought you were a good prospect.

T:

Then why did you treat me like this? Why did you try to keep me out?

P:

You kept yourself out, Mr. Thomas.

T: *Defeated.*
Is that it, then? You're not going to let me in?

P: *Politely rising.*
No, Mr. Thomas.

T:

I see. Is that . . . you know, final?

P:

Yes. Quite.

T:

Slowly rising to retrieve his coat and hat.
You know, you've got me wrong.

P:

I only asked the questions. The answers were yours.

T:

That's the trick, isn't it? If I'd been asking the questions . . . if
I'd found out what it was you were after . . .   *He puts his
coat over one arm, carries his hat.*

P:

Yes, Mr. Thomas, that's the trick.

T:

Returning to R. of desk.
Then at least . . . tell me how I failed.

P:

I'm afraid I can't do that.

T:

Sitting as if to stay.
No, honestly, tell me where I went wrong.

P:

I wish I could, but it's against the rules.

T:

Flaring, banging his hat on the desk.
I know what it is! The whole thing's been a blind! You never
intended to let me in the first place, isn't that it?

P: *Still standing behind his desk.*
Please, Mr. Thomas. I've been very patient . . .

T:

It's my religion, isn't it! — even though I said I'd be anything
you liked.

P:

I swear to you it has nothing to do with religion.

T: *Rising, facing him.*
Then what is it? Race? Class? You blackball people — that's
it, isn't it? — and I don't fit because I never could fit, because
I didn't pick the right parents to fit into this bloody
place!   *Angrily throws his coat into the chair.*

P:

You're being very unpleasant.

T:

You bet!

P:

It has nothing to do with religion, race, class . . .

T:

Oh, no! It never has! Hasn't anything to do with money either,
has it! 'We don't have a means test here,' eh? Oh, no! Nothing
like that . . . only you ask a whole lot of red herrings so you never
do have to have a means to test — you just blackball people and
tell them they don't say the right answers — what's red and blue,
for God's sake!

P:

I wish I could convince you —

T:

Well, I don't want to get in!   *Picking up his coat.*   I
wouldn't come in if you paid me! I wouldn't set foot in this hell
hole if it was the last, you know, resting place on earth!

P:

Have you finished?

T: *Down.*
Yes. I'm finished.

P: *Extends his hand.*
      Good-bye then, Mr. Thomas.   *No response: drops his arm.*   I'm sorry you feel the way you do, but there it is.   *Takes envelope from drawer.*

T:
      I'm . . . I'm sorry too. But after . . . when a man's, you know, been counting on something, you ought to tell him why. You owe him that much.

P: *Inserting into the envelope a cheque which he detaches from the document.*
      I'm afraid we owe you nothing, Mr. Thomas, except the deposit.   *He hands the envelope to T.*

T: *Taking it, but not pocketing it.*
      You won't tell me?

P:
      Sorry.

T:
      Well, thanks.   *Puts envelope in pocket; picks up hat.*

P:
      Not at all. You can find your own way out?   *If there is a door, he opens it.*

T:
      Yes, I can find my way out.   *Crosses to door, turns back, extends hand.*   Well, forgive me for asking.

P:
      What did you say?

T:
      I said, forgive me.

P:
      I was hoping you'd say that.   *Shakes his hand.*   Work on that, Mr. Thomas, and try us again in a few years. If you're

still around. And if we're still around. As you say, one can never tell what'll happen. Perhaps when you've learned to accept yourself . . .

T:

Thanks.   *Puts on hat.*

P:

Good-bye for now, then, Mr. Thomas.

T:

Good-bye for now.

> *T. goes. If there is a door, P. closes it. P. crosses back to his desk, opens the file drawer, inserts the document, closes the drawer. Then he flicks the light switch on the side of his desk, and — the LIGHTS GO OUT.*

THE ARGUMENT

a play in one act

Persons in the play:
  M, a man
  W, a woman

An early radio version of "The Argument" was presented by the Canadian Broadcasting Corporation in 1970. An unperformed stage version, published in *Performing Arts Magazine*, then led to a television production by the British Broadcasting Corporation in 1972. Produced by Tim Aspinall and directed by Brian Farnham for "Thirty Minute Theatre," this version starred Judy Parfitt as the Woman and Lee Montague as the Man. That production in turn led to this revised version for the stage.

The play takes place in the present in any domestic interior or exterior in which a man and a woman — here of unspecified age and relationship, but living together — have just finished dinner. Given a certain level of maturity on both sides, the dialogue could take place between husband and wife, lovers, brother and sister, father and daughter, mother and son. The scene may be done in this way as an exercise in ambiguity; but it is also designed to allow the same pair of actors to perform the scene in consecutive variations, each showing a different relationship in a different social context.

Stage directions and vernacular expressions should be varied accordingly. But in all cases the action must form a counterpoint to the dialogue, each independently following its own internal logic. The after-meal action is a highly patterned ritual; the argument is an apparently spontaneous eruption during which the participants cling for security to this ritual, however unrelated (or mockingly related) to the discourse. But the argument arises because the time is ripe, and takes on a life of its own. The issues are incidental.

> *Finishing their dinner, the MAN and the WOMAN silently rise and leave the table. As she begins to clear away the remnants, he retires to a comfortable chair and switches on the television set.*

W:

Are you listening to me?

M:

Yes, I'm listening.

W:

You're not listening.   *She leaves, carrying things to the kitchen, off.*

> *A pause. He starts to flip channels.*

W: *Returning.*
Every time I try to talk about things, I mean really talk about them, you bury your head in that damn thing.

M:

How am I supposed to know when you want to talk? Why now?

W:

Didn't hear a word I said! Like talking to a chair. *Goes off.*

M:

I'm not really watching; I'm looking, if you don't mind, to see if there's anything *worth* watching.

W: *Off.*
Why lie about it?

M: *Shouting.*
I'm not lying!

W: *Returning.*
When did you stop?

M:

When did you become a lawyer?

W:

I don't want to start an argument.

M:

Then don't.

W:

ɪ I want to talk to you. Can't we just talk about something without starting an argument?

M:

It's up to you. Just don't start off by calling me a liar.

> *She looks at him, then goes silently off to the kitchen. He goes back to television, watches for a moment, then turns it off.*

M:

What do you want to talk about?

W: *Off.*
You know damn well what I want to talk about.

M:
Then why am I asking?

W: *Returning.*
You don't want to talk about it, so you pretend you don't know
what it is, so I have to bring it up, and you can accuse me of
starting an argument.

M:
I didn't accuse you of anything, for Christ's sake! You accused
me of lying!   *He picks up a pipe and prepares to smoke.*

        A pause; they study each other.

W:
You've always been a liar.

M:
Oh, you know that as a fact, do you!

W:
It's not just me. Richard told me that.

M:
Richard told you that?

W:
He knows you better than anyone.   *Goes off to kitchen with
something.*

M: *Up.*
I know him too. He's jealous. Been jealous of me all his life!
He'd say anything to get back at me — especially if it makes
you happy.

W: *Off.*
He can't understand how you got away with it.

M: *Relaxed; on top of it.*
Damn right he can't. That's why he's jealous!

W: *Returning.*
You admit it.

M:

Admit what?

W: *Removing table coverings and putting them away.*
That you're not to be trusted.

M:

I admit Richard's not to be trusted when he's talking to anybody about me, especially you. You want to be a lawyer, don't listen to hearsay.

W:

I don't have to. You lied to me just now — to my face.

M:

You mean about not watching?

W:

You lie to me all the time. I don't need an outside opinion.

M:

You wouldn't listen to an honest one if you got it.

W:

You told me you had enough money in the bank to buy that car. *She sails off into the kitchen.*

M:

Now what! *Angrily pursuing her offstage:* I didn't say I had enough to buy it. I said I had enough for the down payment. That's an expensive number. I'd never've —

W: *Off.*
Not a word about a down payment — not a word.

M: *Off.*
May I finish? With respect! . . . I *meant* I had enough for a down payment, and with what I'm expecting from the Centre —

W: *Off.*
Are you going to drag *that* in again.

M: *Off.*
I'm not dragging it in — it's the reason I may be able —

W: *Off.*
The Centre, the Centre! When? when? Oh, you're so childish!

        The slam of a pot on a table.

M: *Off.*
Oh well, if you won't listen —!

W: *Returning with coffee cup.*
I listened the first time. And you said —

M: *Following her in with his.*
I know what I meant: okay? Whatever you think I said, why should I have said something I didn't mean?

W: *Setting her cup down.*
I'm not a mind reader, you know.   *She returns to the kitchen with his ashtray.*

M:

You're not even a lip-reader. I know what I said — but *you:* see no good, hear no good, speak no good. And what the hell has the car got to do with anything? I probably won't get it — I'm just thinking about it. Okay? Jesus.

        He sits. She returns with the clean ashtray. He lays the pipe in it.

M:

If you want to come and talk, come and talk — I can't carry on a conversation with a revolving garbage can.

149

W:

You revolve and I'll sit.

M:

Tomorrow.

>   *She picks up something to work at while she sits. Later she will tidy, dust, polish, sort, possibly iron, vacuum, etc.*

W:

Lies and fantasies. You live on fantasies, and when they don't work out, you lie your way out of it.

M:

They don't all not work out.

W:

First the dreams, then the lies.

M:

Where would both of us be now if I didn't dream up ways of making a living?

W:

I might be better off — not running around picking up after you.

M:

Now who's dreaming? You want some kind of job? Is that what's bothering you? We'll trade: I do the dishes, you pay the bills.

W:

I don't know what I am, anymore: mother, wife, daughter, sister, companion . . .

M:

Is that my fault?

W: *After a loaded look.*
You told me that woman meant nothing to you.

M:

Oh, I see! Now we come down to it. *Lord of the manor, he rises to rove, playing in turn with each of his obedient toys: a musical instrument, trophies, books, game-boards, etc.* That's not *quite* what I said.

W:

I have a very good memory. Then when I asked you another time you said you remembered her with some affection.

M: *Judicious, judicial.*

May I point out, with respect, that there's nothing mutually exclusive about those statements? The first was in reply to a question about having sex.. Thanks but no thanks. I told you she meant nothing to me and I meant exactly that. The second remark, as I recall, was in the middle of a discussion on human nature in general — one of your favourite topics — and we finally got down to hers in particular. In *that* context I said I remembered her with some — *some* — affection, because I thought she was fun. That's all.

W:

She's a slut.

M:

That's what you say.

W:

A common slut.

M:

Have it your way.

W:

She would have brought you nothing but trouble.

M:

You never met her, but don't let that stop you.

W:

And you remember her with affection.

M:

I said *some* affection. Don't put words into my mouth, and don't take them out, either.

W:

Some affection means affection, doesn't it?

M:

Some is any amount — could be very little. It's ambiguous.

W:

And that's how you intended it.

M:

No —!

W:

I'm supposed to think 'not much' while you think 'plenty.'

M:

Think whatever you like, which is what you'll do anyway. *I'm* not ambiguous — words are. But they're all we've got to talk with. If you want to argue, you have to argue with words. It's like a clothesline — has to be held up at two ends. Doesn't matter where the line starts; if you tie it onto your hook it'll end up in a different place than if I tie it onto mine. That's a simple enough principle; you know all about clotheslines.

W:

All that song means is you want to have it both ways.

M:

Jesus. I was trying to convey . . . There's a limit to what words do.

W:

Oh.

M:

I can't help it if the phrase isn't precise enough. Some means some, and that's all it means.

W:

Something is not the same as nothing.

M:

Who said it was! Can we leave it at that?

A pause.

W:

The *third* time you said there must have been something to the relationship.

M: *Pouncing.*
I did not — you did. You said for any relationship to occur there must have been something to it. I mean . . . !

W:

You mean there wasn't?

M:

Look! There is, I suppose, a sense in which a relationship between two objects, since it exists, may be said to have something to it. But I didn't say what, because I wasn't interested in analysing it at the time, not having you around to interrogate me, and so I don't *know* what.

W:

You don't remember: is that it?

M:

I don't go around remembering it, licking it over like a broken tooth, no! Can we get this straight? We were talking — you were talking, that last time — about *learning* from relationships, even negative relationships, and I was *agreeing*, that's all, that if you learn something there must've been something there to learn from.

W:

Affection, in this case.

M: *Through clenched teeth.*
Some! In the sense of not much!

     A substantial pause.

W:

How much?

M:

What do you want: a slide rule? A goldsmith's scales? I didn't
even say what I remembered her with, whenever I remember
her at all, which is only as often as you bring it up.   *In
his anger he breaks something and sits.*

W: *Having allowed him to subside.*
Have you made up your mind yet? Which version is the true
one? That's the one I'm interested in. This is a new one — that
you don't remember her. Or it's something you didn't quite say,
or didn't quite mean when you said it. Which one do I believe?

M:

They're your versions, not mine. And will you please tell me
what the hell it matters now? If you ferret and ferret till you're
blue in the face, you weren't there, you can't know anything
for sure, and all you're ever going to get is what I tell you —
take it or leave it. If you were God almighty and had all the
evidence in front of your nose — exhibits A, B and C plucked
from the scene of the crime and laid out on the table — what
the hell would it matter now?

W:

It matters whether you tell the truth or not.

M: *Laughing ruefully.*
Oh Jesus, it doesn't seem to! You know, I'll tell you how your
mind works: put him in the witness-box over and over, when
he least suspects it — I mean, start by talking about television,
or Richard or the car or something, so he won't have his guard
up — and get him to answer the same question over and over
with a slight change in emphasis so you can accuse him of lying
the time before. That's what you try to do.

W:

Who has to try? You keep changing your story. I want the facts.

M:

The hell you do! Facts aren't good enough for you. You only want magic numbers to prove whatever screwy idea you had in the first place — and you won't be satisfied till you get them. Don't give me that!

W:

I want the simple truth.

M:

The truth isn't simple!

W:

Not for you it isn't.

M:

Arggh! *Bursting into pained laughter:* Can't you see what you're doing? Trying to *make* it simple, forcing every event, every person, into your damn pigeon-hole, you kill the very truth you're looking for! Can't you see that?

W:

I can see you're good at twisting.

M:

I'm twisting?

W:

If everything's nice and vague and can't be pinned down, then neither can you. 'What is truth?' said Pontius Pilate, and washed his hands.

M:

Pontius Pilate, for Christ's sake, was fed up with the local priests and their hairsplitting. Hairsplitting — that's what he was washing his hands of.

W:

And look what came of it.

M:

Well I'm washing my hands of yours.

W:

According to you I can never get at the facts, so we might as well let the whole thing drop.

M:

Exactly.   *Pause.*   It's no skin off your nose, you know.

Another, longer pause, while they study each other.

W:

It would be if at your age you made . . . other arrangements.

M:

What are you talking about?

W:

You know what I'm talking about.

M:

I don't know what you're talking about. What are you onto now?

W:

You weren't listening, then.

M:

I heard you. What 'other arrangements' are you talking about?

W:

You know what other arrangements I'm talking about.

M:

So help me God, I wouldn't put it past you to trump up this whole argument, to justify 'other arrangements' for yourself. What've you got in mind?

W:

So you have been considering the possibility.

M:

What possibility? That I might walk out on you, or you might walk out on me?

W:

You — with that slut.

M:

Jesus.   *He rises to pace again; grimly.*   It's all past. I'm not interested in whatever you think happened. You can't rewrite it, no matter how hard you try, and I wish you'd forget it.

W:

I'm sure you do — it'd suit you to a tee. Except that then I'd never be sure you were telling the truth, even now, and that's what matters.

M:

Ah! The light goes on! What I hear you saying is that facts don't matter, that you don't really care what happened so long as you're convinced I'm telling the truth. Is that it?

W:

I've been saying it for half an hour.

M:

God give me patience. All right: I admit it. I murdered the woman. Strangled her with her own scarf.

W:

What's the use!

M:

You don't believe me: see! I murdered ten women. I robbed a bank. I blew up the airport. I poisoned the water supply with strychnine I bought out of profits from selling drugs to schoolkids. Now I take it none of this is really rotten so long as I come and tell you. Is that right?

W:

No, because I wouldn't believe you.

M:

You don't believe me anyway!

W:

Because you tell such awful lies.

M:

Jesus. What do you want me to do: confess my sins to you every day, like a priest? — because it's obvious my sins are all you're interested in.

W:

I'm interested in the truth.

M:

The hell you are! You're a newspaper: you're only interested in the truth if it stinks. It doesn't matter to you what the facts are — you've just finished saying that — so long as I bring you enough ugly bits to convince you I'm not leaving them out.

W:

You can't face the ugly bits, can you?

M:

If it's fact and not fantasy I'll face it.

W:

Then why not come right out and admit you lied to get your job.

M: *Reeling.*
What? When! What are you talking about?

W:

Admit you lied to get that job.

M:

Could you possibly stick to the subject — for at least thirty seconds? My job, if you insist on switching horses in midstream

— and the way you switch I'm amazed you ever get from one side to the other — I got my job the usual way: I applied and they hired me.

W:

You misled them.

M:

The hell I did.

W:

Told them you were an accountant.

M:

I've kept books, haven't I? That's all I said.

W:

You mean half a truth is better than none.

M:

I mean I don't go around telling people more than they need to know, when they're perfectly satisfied.

W:

With half the truth.

M:

With the *necessary* half.

W:

Tell a half-truth and blame somebody else if they believe the other half.

M:

They didn't believe the other half!

W:

But when *I* do . . .

M:

When you do what?

W:

Believe the half you think is unnecessary.

M:

About keeping books?

W:

About that woman. Why can't you say she's a slut.

M:

Because that's your word, not mine.

W:

Then she isn't a slut?

M:

Here we go! Black or white! A or Z with nothing in between. You could've made a fortune as a lawyer.

W:

Are you refusing to answer the question on the grounds that it might incriminate you?

M:

I refuse to answer any question that incriminates me any way I answer it. Why not ask me if the world is flat or square?

W:

Because it's round.

M:

It isn't — that's the whole point. It isn't *quite* round. It even changes its shape, for God's sake.

W:

You love arguing by analogy, don't you! Saves you from coping with your own personality.

M:

I can cope with mine. It's yours I can't cope with.

W:

Because I make you face yourself.

M:

Look.   *Making a great effort to be reasonable.*   I say something. Okay. You put your own interpretation on it, put a little frame around it, hang it on the wall, and it becomes a mantra, like 'God Bless Our Little Home.' Your piece of embroidery becomes Holy Writ. The thesis becomes the topic. Do you mind this lesson in logic? I mean, it doesn't offend your female intuition?

W:

Go right ahead. I'll let you know.

M:

Thank you.

W:

Not at all.

M:

So with your thesis established, you take another statement of mine, torn from another context, and call it the antithesis. From thesis and antithesis — both, you'll note, transformed by your delicate embroidery — you proceed to a synthesis. But this brilliant little effect is entirely your own invention from start to finish, so what comes out is concentrated hogwash. And I'm the poor bastard who's accused of lying!

W:

Thanks for the lesson.   *She rises, puts away what she has been working at, and turns her attention to another domestic chore.*   The trouble is, I only know what you've told me. Or did I make that up too?

M:

You didn't necessarily make it up, you made it different: Some of it up, some of it down, some of it out, some of it off . . . a little twist here, a little bend there . . .

W:

Smug, aren't you.

M:

Smug?

W:

Men thinking they're being logical.

M:

You don't have any faith in logic?

W:

I don't have any faith in men!

M:

Oh! Ah! Well, now! Down to the heart of the onion, eh! The TV, Richard, the car, the person you invariably refer to as a slut, my job, my personality — peel them off, one by one! The preliminaries are over — we're down to the main bout. Jesus.

W:

I don't think the subject's changed at all.

M:

Oh, I can see that now! Now I can see this is what you've been leading up to all the time: You hate men!

W:

No I don't. I just don't trust them.

M:

All men?

W:

Certain aspects of all men.

M:

Oh come on, now! The way your mind works, it has to be all or nothing — no sliding scale, no spectrum. I guess all men are bastards, eh?

W:

A lot of the time.

M:

Or sons of bitches?

W:

Just doing our job.

M:

All women are virtuous, right!

W:

A lot of the time.

M:

A woman only does bad things when a man does something bad
to her.

W:

You don't like that idea, do you!

M:

Like it? What's that got to do with it? It's bullshit.

W:

Even your language.

M:

You've been saving this up, haven't you! While I'm out working
my ass off, you've been stocking up, hoarding ammunition to
fire off at me the minute we finish dinner and I sit down for ten
minutes. Ambush him. Shoot him when he's unarmed. Hit him
with all the latest feminist bullshit.

W:

Lower and lower.

M:

Talk about trusting!

W:

Listen to yourself: ammunition, fire off, shoot, hit — bull talk!

M:

All men are bastards and all women are angels: right?

W:

Now who's putting words in whose mouth?

M:

Maybe I didn't hear you correctly.

W:

Who's playing variations now!

M:

You said men are liars.

W:

I meant it.

M:

That's what you mean?

W:

No, I meant it then.

M:

Jesus.

W:

And I might mean it again. I'm hearing your real voice now, but you've got a bad case history.

M:

Who's got a bad case history?

W:

Men. The hunters. The great rationalizers.

M:

You've been watching some program.

W:

You beat up the next man, then the next town, then the next tribe, then the next country, then any old country, then visitors from outer space. You make a mess of the world with war, and when you get tired of war you make a mess of nature. And all the time you dream up the most beautiful excuses for the mess, while we come along and clean it up.

M: *Almost speechless with rage.*
What the hell have you been reading? Who do you think we do it for?

W:

Yourselves.

M:

Women never played any part in this? They got nothing out of it?

W:

Not much.

M:

They didn't cheer us on, they didn't eat the food we dragged in, they didn't wear the fur coats, sit in the houses, spend our money?

W:

More bull talk. Women work.

M:

They don't drive cars, they don't throw garbage into the river?

W:

And all the time we look after the children.

M:

Christ, who's rationalizing now! It was all for the sake of the children. Including the boys — don't forget that. All these little hunters, brought up by women. Why didn't you teach them to be good little girls?

W:

Because God was a man.

M:

Of course! If we'd had a woman in charge there'd be nothing but sweetness and light.

W:

Could it be any worse?

M:

Jesus Christ, I don't know. She sits there in good health, at home, no real problems, not a serious care in the world, and asks if it could be any worse.

W:

Do you think that's all there is?

M:

Where do you get clangers like that? 'Do you think that's all there is!' Happiness is a warm puppy; happiness is kids singing; happiness is looove — I can tell you one thing: happiness for me is not being told I'm a liar and a bastard because I'm programmed that way.

W:

What's happiness for you?   *She sits.*

M:

Coming back from a hard day's work without a harpy at the door. Not getting slapped with a writ right after dinner.

W:

That's all I am, isn't it: a welcome mat.   *Incipient tears.*

M: *Repentent.*
No. No, it isn't. Who said anything about a mat?

W:

That's all I've been to you all these years.

M: *Gently.*
Now wait a minute . . .

W:

You didn't notice, because you didn't want to notice. You don't even remember.

M:

Remember what?

W:

You don't even know what I'm talking about.

M:

I wish to hell I did.

W:

We can't even talk any more.

M:

I'll talk if you'll tell me what we're supposed to be talking about.

W:

You don't remember. But you remember her.

M:

Who?

W:

That slut. You remember her with affection.

M: *Kindly.*
Are we going to go through all that again? Look: I'm not a mental telepathist.

W:

We used to be close enough to share thoughts.

M:

Just tell me what's bugging you.

W:

You were sitting there watching TV . . .

M:

And you wanted me to do the dishes? Just ask. That's all you have to do: ask.

W:

You weren't even listening.

M:

I was listening.

W: *Rising, back in command.*
All right: what did I say?

M:

You said I was a liar. I was convicted of being a man. Without a hearing.

W:

Before that.

M:

At dinner?

W:

At dinner.

M:

Something about a trip?

W:

And you weren't listening.

M:

I was. You just heard me say so.

W:

You didn't say anything.

M:

What was there to say?

W:

You didn't say what you thought about it.

M:

Well, I mean, what does it matter? We don't always have to go together.

W:

You've always arranged our trips before, always played the man.

M: *Wryly.*
Oh — you want me to be more aggressive.

W:

Don't you care where I go?

M:

I care a lot.

W: *Suddenly hardening, breaking away.*
You're lying again!

M:

You know something? — you're impossible! God damn impossible! *Flaring:* I get hell for lying and hell for telling the truth. I get hell for acting like a man and hell for not acting like one. It doesn't matter what I do, it couldn't matter less what I say, you're out to destroy me.

W: *Needling him.*
You're contradicting yourself with every word you speak. Now where's your precious logic!

M:

Yours is driving me out of my mind, I'll tell you that!

W: *Ferociously.*

Go on! Now we're getting the truth! Go on telling me how impossible I am, how life is hell for you here with me, how I'm driving you out of your mind! What that proves is not what you think, but that *you*'ve made up your mind about *me*! It won't work any longer, will it!

He raises his fists in speechless rage.

W:

Come on! Threaten me! You don't know how to do anything else!

He strikes her. She reacts with a tight cry of triumph. He is bewildered by his own action, and groans. A long pause. Lost, he breaks contact and goes to sit. She briskly collects the coffee cups and removes them to the kitchen. She returns, and stands looking at him.

M:

If you went away . . .

W:

A trip. I said a trip, that's all.

M:

Don't go.

W:

We'll see.   *She sits and begins to knit, smiling.*

THE LIGHTS FADE

Come Away, Come Away

a play in one act

Persons in the play:
  An Old Man
  A Young Girl

"Come Away, Come Away" was first produced in 1972, in a version for radio, by the Canadian Broadcasting Corporation, in the series "CBC Tuesday Night." The Old Man was played by Mavor Moore, the Young Girl by Karen Pearson. The program was directed by Jean Bartels, with music by Morris Surdin, played by Neville Barnes.

A film was made in 1973, produced by George Jonas for the Canadian Broadcasting Corporation television series "Program X." The film was directed by Bob Shultz. The Old Man was played by George Waight, and the Young Girl by Julie McNall.

A wooded park near a city. Late afternoon in autumn; golden sunshine. A big maple tree, a favourite for climbers, shelters a bench. We hear sound-scraps of birds singing, dogs barking, children playing, lovers laughing. Then, in the far distance, a mournful, unrhythmical guitar.

Along a path strides a well-dressed old man, drinking it in, his cane more like a swagger stick than a crutch. He pokes among the leaves, then sits on the bench and half dozes. A little girl enters, in bare feet and simply dressed, carrying a large brown-paper shopping bag. She studies him for a moment before speaking.

GIRL:
> Hi.

OLD MAN:
> Mm? Oh, hello there.   *Pause.*

GIRL:
> I'm collecting leaves.

OLD MAN:
> Yes, I can see that.   *Pause.*

GIRL:
> They're all dead.

OLD MAN:
> Yes. Used to be green; then they turn red and stay on the tree for their picture and then they die.

GIRL:
> That's when they fall down.

OLD MAN:
> Oh, yes, that's what happens.   *Pause.*

GIRL:
> What are *you* doing?

OLD MAN:

Me? Well, I was thinking.

GIRL:

Hmph.

OLD MAN:

It may not sound like much, but there's a good deal to thinking.

GIRL:

Is it harder 'n reading?

OLD MAN:

Oh, much. Reading, somebody else gives you the ideas. Thinking, you have to come up with them yourself.

GIRL:

How do you?

OLD MAN:

Well, at first you have to have a lot to think about. That means you have to have done a lot.

GIRL:

You mean lived?

OLD MAN:

Yes, that's it. Then you have to remember it. Now that's not easy, remembering.

GIRL:

I remember lots of things.

OLD MAN:

Oh, well, that's because you haven't got all that much to work on yet. I have boxes and boxes and files and cabinets and shelves and cupboards — right here in my head. Yes. Someday I'll get them all sorted out, you know . . . but right now I flip open my mind, and out pops a thought — then another. You put one thought up against the next and they dance together, and the two of them make you think of another — and pretty soon there's a whole roomful of thoughts, all shapes and sizes, a whole fancy dress ball — and you lose sight of the thought you started with, because all you can see is the pattern they make, like a crazy quilt, only moving, moving.

GIRL:
Like leaves?

OLD MAN:
Yes.   *Pause.*   Only it's one after the other, you see. Like notes that make a tune, and pretty soon you've forgotten the notes and only remember the tune. And the tune comes back and back, and you forget where it started. Echoes.

GIRL:
Hmph.

Pause.

OLD MAN:
Then you have to start remembering again.

GIRL:
What're you remembering?

OLD MAN:
Oh, times.

GIRL:
Hmph.

Pause.

OLD MAN:
You all alone?

GIRL:
Sure.

OLD MAN:
You live near here?

GIRL:
Nope.

OLD MAN:
Far away?

GIRL: *Moving offstage.*
Quite a way.

OLD MAN:
Why'd you come so far?

GIRL: *Off.*
I told you. The leaves.

OLD MAN:
Oh, yes.   *Pause.*   You come here often?

GIRL: *Off.*
Sure. Do you?

OLD MAN:
Sometimes. I've never seen you before.

GIRL: *Off.*
I've seen you.

OLD MAN:
My eyes aren't as good as they used to be.

GIRL: *Off.*
Does it make you remember, coming here?

OLD MAN:
Yes. But no; not really. Nothing ever happened to me here. I
mean, I never came here when I was a kid, like you. I had
another place, far away. I used to climb trees, swing on the
branches and the vines, chase chipmunks. Oh, I was a great tree
climber!

GIRL: *Off.*
  Why d'you come here?

OLD MAN:
  Oh, I don't know . . . this place: gives me new things to think
  about — new things that're really old too, like streams and
  pebbles and flowers, only in new patterns. You need to smell
  things growing, changing. Things getting ready to happen —
  right on the brink, not over and done with. Otherwise . . . you
  see, it's wondering — wondering what's going to happen — that
  keeps you alive. Touching things, young people,
  wondering.   *Pause.*   Old people talk too much.

GIRL: *Off.*
  Hey!

OLD MAN:
  What?

GIRL: *Coming onstage.*
  Look — I found something! In the leaves, all covered with leaves!

OLD MAN:
  What's that you've got?

GIRL:
  A dead bird.

OLD MAN:
  What's it, a sparrow?

        Pause.

GIRL:
  It won't ever fly again.

OLD MAN:
  Best put it down.

        The GIRL stubbornly deposits it in her bag.

OLD MAN:

> Better bury him when you get home.

GIRL:

> He's all stiff.

OLD MAN:

> Yes. You get like that. Yes.　　*Pause.*　　You know that
> fellow who plays the guitar?

GIRL:

> Sure. He plays it all the time.

OLD MAN:

> Sometimes I hear him, sometimes I don't. My ears aren't all
> that good now.

GIRL:

> He makes it up.

OLD MAN:

> Yes.　　*Pause.*　　Is he a young fellow?

GIRL:

> No. He's sad.

OLD MAN:

> Still . . . how do you know?

GIRL:

> He told me.

OLD MAN:

> You talk to everybody?

GIRL:

> If they like to.

OLD MAN:

> You're not scared?

GIRL:

    Nope.

OLD MAN:

    You're not scared of me?

GIRL:

    Nope.   *Empties her bag on the ground.*

OLD MAN:

    Well, now.   *Pause.*   That's nice, that's very nice.   *Pause.*   What're you doing now?

GIRL:

    Sorting the leaves.

OLD MAN:

    That'll take a long time.

GIRL:

    I know.

OLD MAN:

    And you don't mind talking to me?

GIRL:

    Nope.

OLD MAN:

    Your mother never tell you not to talk to strangers?

GIRL:

    Why not?

OLD MAN:

    Well . . . old men. Lonely old men.

GIRL:

    How old are you?

OLD MAN:
> Oh, I'm pretty old.

GIRL:
> How old?

OLD MAN:
> Over eighty. How old are you?

GIRL:
> Why d'you want to know?

OLD MAN: *Mock umbrage.*
> I told you *my* age!

GIRL:
> Guess.

OLD MAN:
> Well, I'd say . . . about seven. And a half.

> *Pause.*

GIRL:
> How old are the leaves?

OLD MAN:
> These ones? Oh, maybe six months.

GIRL:
> Hmph.

OLD MAN:
> So you see you're older than they are, and I'm a lot older than you are — and we can all talk together, and nobody's scared of anybody else! *He suddenly laughs.* Say, it does me good to talk to you! Think of all you've got ahead of you! I like you! What's your name?

GIRL:
> Oh, people call me different.

OLD MAN:

What do you call yourself?

GIRL:

All depends.

OLD MAN:

Depends on what?

GIRL:

What I'm doing.

OLD MAN:

What do you call yourself when you're out sorting and cheering up an old man?

GIRL:

Lee.

OLD MAN:

Lee? That's a boy's name!

GIRL:

Not just.

OLD MAN:

I never heard of a girl called Lee.   *Sighs.*   I don't know — I like girls' names better. I had a granddaughter, name of Millie.   *Pause.*   Crying. That fellow used to hit her. No good. Still, what could anyone do? I told him, right out. Said, you're piling up grief. Blamed everyone but himself. Tears streaming down her face. Do you love him, Millie? It killed her.   *He groans.*

GIRL:

You got something wrong with you?

OLD MAN:

Mm? Something wrong?

GIRL:

Old people always have something wrong with them.

OLD MAN:

Oh, that.

GIRL:

Then what?

OLD MAN:

Oh well . . . I'm not too bad.

The GIRL starts to refill her bag.

GIRL:

Do you hurt?

OLD MAN:

Not so's you'd notice.

GIRL:

Don't you hurt *somewhere?*

OLD MAN:

Well, now and then.

GIRL:

Where?

OLD MAN:

Places.

GIRL:

All over?

OLD MAN:

Sometimes.

GIRL:

That what happens when you get old?

OLD MAN:
> That's about it. That's about it.

> *The guitar in the distance stops.*

GIRL:
> Has it stopped now?

OLD MAN:
> What?

GIRL:
> The hurt.

OLD MAN:
> Some.

GIRL: *Moving away.*
> You were remembering, weren't you!

OLD MAN:
> Yes.   *Pause.*   That's what happens, you see. I was thinking about you . . .

GIRL:
> When I came over?

OLD MAN:
> Just now . . .

GIRL:
> I saw you looking at me.

OLD MAN:
> I was, and then . . .

GIRL:
> I saw you look away. You didn't even see the water or the trees or anything.

OLD MAN:

> That's what happens. There's a difference, what you see and what you're looking at.

GIRL:

> How come?

OLD MAN:

> Well, you now, you think of what you're doing, you look at what you're seeing, at leaves. I think of what I'm looking at on the inside of my head. That's because I'm old.

GIRL:

> You shortsighted?

OLD MAN:

> A funny thing, that. When you get old, you grow four eyes.

GIRL:

> Four?

OLD MAN:

> Yes. The two you started with get weaker, but then you grow two more that get stronger.

GIRL:

> Show me.

OLD MAN:

> Oh, you can't see them. One's on the inside, so's you can see your whole life, like movies, the best bits and the scary bits . . . get you all excited again . . . so you can be sure they really happened or couldn't have happened . . .

GIRL:

> Where's the other eye?

OLD MAN:

> It's outside somewhere, away out, at the end of a long arm, like a periscope, looking back at you, so you see yourself and everything you're doing and can't stop yourself doing.

GIRL:

Like what?

OLD MAN:

Oh, talking. You hear other old people talking your ear off, and you swear you won't be like that, but you talk. And crying for no reason. Putting your feet where you don't want them to go. Telling people you love to go to blazes. Throwing things out you want to keep and keeping things you want to throw out. Remembering. Most of all, remembering.

GIRL:

Don't you like remembering?

OLD MAN:

Some things. Oh yes, some things you . . . but once it starts to work, you see, you can't turn it off . . . things come piling in . . . *He shivers.*

GIRL:

Things you want to forget?

OLD MAN:

Yes. You think forgetting's easy?

GIRL:

Sure. I forget all the time.

OLD MAN:

That's because you haven't all that much to remember. Forgetting's hard, hardest thing there is.

GIRL:

Harder than thinking?

OLD MAN:

Oh, yes. Because to think you have to forget an awful lot. An awful lot, to think straight. It's gone, you see — all gone. Nothing you can do about it, any of it: the people, the times, the places . . . good, bad, or indifferent . . . they're gone. And you can't live in the past. You have to look around you, what's happening now. There's an ache . . . you can't ache it over again. You need . . . new aches . . . to be alive.

Pause.

GIRL:
Is that what you've got now?

OLD MAN:
Talking to you?

GIRL:
You got an ache?

OLD MAN: *Chuckling.*
No! No, you make me feel better.

GIRL:
I made you think how old you were, didn't I?

A long pause; the Old Man is deeply hurt. The Girl turns to picking dead flowers.

GIRL:
You got an ache now?

OLD MAN:
Yes, I . . . is that why you wanted to talk to me?

GIRL:
I just wondered.

OLD MAN: *Gradually recovering, chuckling.*
That's it! That's better! Wondering! Full of wonder! By George! Wonder — that's the cure! That's life — not to know what's coming next and to care, to wonder! Listen, my name's Fred. We're good friends now, aren't we!

GIRL:
Maybe.

OLD MAN:

Oh, I can tell you lots of things! I can show you things —

GIRL:

What did you used to do, before?

OLD MAN: *Eagerly.*

Oh, lots of things. I was a soldier once.

GIRL:

You get wounded?

OLD MAN:

Oh, yes.

GIRL:

Where?

OLD MAN:

You can't see it.

GIRL:

Show me.

OLD MAN:

I'll show you one. *Rolling up his sleeve.*

GIRL:

What made it?

OLD MAN:

A bullet.

GIRL:

Hmph. Who were you fighting?

OLD MAN:

Germans. It was a long time ago.

GIRL:

You kill any of them?

OLD MAN:
Oh, yes. I got a medal for that.

GIRL:
Why?

OLD MAN:
Well, they were trying to kill me.

GIRL:
Why?

OLD MAN:
I forget. But they started it.

GIRL:
You didn't do anything?

OLD MAN:
I don't think so. Not right then. Not first.

GIRL:
Did you hate them?

OLD MAN:
Oh, yes.

GIRL:
Was that why you killed them?

OLD MAN:
I guess so.

GIRL:
You have to hate somebody to kill them?

OLD MAN:
Oh, yes. Otherwise . . .

GIRL:
Did the man who shot at you hate you?

OLD MAN:

    I guess he must've.

GIRL:

    You always hate someone who kills you?

OLD MAN:

    Well, it's too late after. You have to hate them first.

GIRL:

    But why?

OLD MAN:

    I don't know.

GIRL:

    If someone killed you now, would you have to hate them first?

OLD MAN:

    Oh, yes. But no; it all depends. It depends on when.

GIRL:

    Now.

       Pause.

OLD MAN:

    I don't know.

GIRL:

    But you're old now. It wouldn't matter.   *She runs off.*

OLD MAN:

    It's not the ones you hate who die.

GIRL: *Running back in with a bright red leaf.*

    Look at this! You ever see one so beautiful?

OLD MAN:

    All that blood. How could he lie there in the mud and not see a tank plough over him? Over his head. She couldn't face the thought. Fifty years. Fifty years later, she still . . . don't you think *I* dream about it? You think it helps to know you can't forget? He's gone, we're here. Our own lives to live. Making love, how *can* you with a ghost behind the eyes?

GIRL:
Why does the red turn yellow?

OLD MAN:
He's my son, not his. My head.   *Pause.*   For what it's worth. It's not the ones you hate who kill you.

GIRL:
Who, then?

OLD MAN:
And it's not the ones you hate who die.

GIRL:
Who, then?

OLD MAN:
The ones you love. One after the other.

GIRL:
You ever kill someone you love?

OLD MAN:
Oh, yes.   *Pause.*   Once you find where it hurts . . .

GIRL:
What hurts?

Pause.

OLD MAN:
Well, children hurt. Growing hurts. Knowing hurts. The world hurts.

GIRL:
Show me.

OLD MAN:

> How?

GIRL:

Show me the other wounds.

OLD MAN:

> Oh, not mine . . . I can show you mine, but I don't mean them, the ones I carry. It's the ones I . . . the ones others . . . *Pause.*   And they're all gone, you see. You can't ever make it up.

> *This time he walks away; she follows.*

GIRL:

How come, with everybody getting killed and dying, you got to be so old?

OLD MAN:

> Oh, well!   *He laughs and brightens.*   I was lucky, you see — and careful.

GIRL:

What'd you do?

OLD MAN:

> Didn't do anything for the lucky part, except be prepared. But careful? Oh, I tell you, I used to keep in shape! I was a good athlete. Spring and fall I used to run — track and field, broad jump, all that. Summers I swam. Oh, I was a strong swimmer, still am. Still go down to the Y, you know . . . every now and then. Badminton, too. And deck tennis, with a quoit . . . you ever play that?

GIRL:

No.

OLD MAN:

> Oh, that's a great game. Tough — have to be tough for deck tennis if you play it right . . . not that namby-pamby kind. And water polo, that's even tougher . . . have to swim with your legs,

keep your hands free for the ball. That was summers, you know. Then winters, snowshoeing. Nobody does that now . . . all this skiing's what they do now . . . but I used to snowshoe. Miles and miles, up north. Only way you could get some places. Oh, that's a muscle builder! *Pause.* Couldn't do that now. *Pause.* Every morning, winter and summer, used to do deep breathing, fresh air. Oh, that sets you up. *Pause.* Can't do that today.

GIRL:

Is it hard breathing, when you're old?

OLD MAN:

No, sir, not that, it's not me, it's the world. No more fresh air. You can't breathe that muck. I'm in pretty good shape — but the world . . .

The sunlight begins to fade.

GIRL:

That all you did?

OLD MAN:

Oh, no, that was just . . . I went to college, after the war. Learned to be a lawyer. Everybody needs a lawyer, you see, because you have to have laws and nobody else can make 'em out. Oh, I was a good lawyer! Used to do my homework. You do your homework?

GIRL:

Sure.

OLD MAN:

Good for you. Well, I used to do my homework. Then I'd get up in court. 'Objection, my lord! Objection sustained!' *Pause.* Sometimes, of course, I wasn't sustained. But I always put up a good fight. One fellow, bank robber, oh, he was a tough customer — I thought they'd hang him sure. But I was able to get him the benefit of the doubt. Big fellow he was, with blond hair and hands like a blacksmith.

By George!   *Pause.*   Later on, he killed his wife with a crowbar. Nice girl.

Pause.

GIRL:
You didn't help her much.

OLD MAN:
No. But I helped lots of good people. One fellow, a piano tuner, hands mangled in a car accident. He'd never've got a cent, but I took it all the way up on appeal. Never charged him a nickel. Said, that's okay, Billy — I'm not in it for the money. Justice.   *Pause.*   Of course, most of it's the quiet stuff. Dog work. Routine, going in and coming out. Paper: 'Whereas the aforesaid' and 'inasmuch as notwithstanding' and 'do hereby jointly and severally' and 'the party of the first part and the party of the second part' . . . and then bang — the seal. You never know.   *Pause.*   I did *not* work too hard! How can you say that? I'm home as much as most men. Weekends, I take the children out. I don't gamble. I don't drink that much. What do you expect of a man?

Pause.

GIRL:
The sun's going down.

Pause.

OLD MAN:
Yes. She used to say that. Summers, we'd be sitting there, after dinner, and she'd say look, the sun's going down.   *Pause.* Hadn't you best be going home?

GIRL:
I'm not through yet.

OLD MAN:
It'll come up again tomorrow. Now let's you and me talk about

193

tomorrow. Forget all that stuff that happened long ago. Let's think about tomorrow.

GIRL:
All right.

OLD MAN: *Vigorously.*
Tomorrow morning, I'm going to get up early.

GIRL:
What's early?

OLD MAN:
Six o'clock. I'll eat a good breakfast, my usual.

GIRL:
What's that?

OLD MAN:
Oatmeal. Always have my bowl of hot oatmeal. Then I'll get dressed and shave and bring in the paper and read all the day's news. You read the paper?

GIRL:
No.

OLD MAN:
Oh, you ought to read the paper! I'm surprised at you not reading the paper. Nothing like it for keeping on top of things. TV, of course, and the radio for background, but they're more companions. The paper's got it all down, the whole story, not just snippets. Oh, the paper's a great thing for knowing what's going on in the world. I read it all — 'continued on page eight,' all that — financial pages, sports section, women's doings, comics, bridge . . . all except the horoscope — that's nonsense. That's the whole point about the future, not to know it, not to know what's coming up the next day. News! How could it be news if you already knew what was coming? Every day's different. Tomorrow, who knows?

GIRL:

Then what?

OLD MAN:

After the paper? *He falters, afraid.* Well, that's . . . after the paper, I have to decide. Up to the paper, it's the same every day. The paper's the same every day, you know.

GIRL:

I thought you said it was different.

OLD MAN:

Oh, the details change! The details are never the same from one day to the next, for goodness's sake! That keeps you guessing. I mean, there's always a war but each time it's someplace else. Women are always changing their clothes, but you never know what next. *That* never changes! Every day, so far, up to the paper, every day's about the same. Then I . . . then I have to decide what to do. *Pause.* What to do. What to do.

GIRL:

You won't be here tomorrow.

OLD MAN:

Well, I don't know. I haven't made up my mind. Maybe I'll see what's going on in the world.

GIRL:

You said the world hurts.

OLD MAN:

Did I?

GIRL:

A while back.

OLD MAN:

Oh, that's only sometimes. *Firmly.* Actually, I have a great deal to do.

GIRL:
Like what?

OLD MAN:
Responsibilities.

GIRL:
You got a family?

OLD MAN:
Grandchildren, you know. They . . . they sometimes need me.   *Pause.*   Oh, yes, I'm needed . . . now and then. One of them calls me up . . . every so often.   *Pause.* 'Course, we don't talk much, in a movie . . . can't say much in a movie, you know . . . but they like the movie. I'm . . . *Pause.*   Actually, I'm pretty busy even for that. Lot of demands on my time.

GIRL:
What for?

OLD MAN:
Well, things to be sorted. Books, papers, that sort of thing. Boxes and filing drawers, all that. I have to go back over it, sort it out. Important papers.

GIRL:
What about?

OLD MAN:
Oh, business, legal, family stuff.

GIRL:
What good's it?

OLD MAN:
Well, it has to be sorted. Catalogued, you know.

GIRL:
That why you kept it?

OLD MAN:
> No, no. It's important.

GIRL:
> What for?

OLD MAN:
> For me. That's my whole life. It has to be sorted. Nobody else
> to do it. Photographs, newspaper clippings, letters, old letters,
> all that. Letters . . . terrible.

GIRL:
> Why'n't you throw them out, then?

OLD MAN:
> They have to be sorted. Some of them . . .   *Pause.*
> They have to be sorted.

> *The sun is on the horizon: light and shadows.*

GIRL:
> Maybe you won't get round to it.

OLD MAN:
> Oh, yes. Tomorrow morning. I'll do it tomorrow. I've been
> putting it off.

GIRL:
> Why?

OLD MAN:
> Digging.

GIRL:
> What?

OLD MAN:
> It's digging. Digging in the . . . digging up memories. That's
> hard.

GIRL:

    Harder than forgetting?

OLD MAN:

    Oh, yes.

GIRL:

    How come?

OLD MAN:

    Well, it's not just memories, you see — you can forget memories if you try. But with these, there they are; not just what you remember, but what they were . . . what you wrote, what she actually looked like . . . the places. What the words said, what the faces say. Holding things. Happy. *Pause.* There it is. *Pause.* How could I have done that to you? *Pause.* Houses. I never meant . . . *Pause.* I didn't say it right. If I could have seen you, talked to you. *Pause.* What lies! By George, that boy would've made a fortune as a storyteller! 'I was robbed in Times Square last night by three thugs: please send me a hundred bucks.' 'The girl's father will let me off if I donate a thousand bucks to the cause.' 'Helen says she'll keep quiet about the drugs if you'll give her the house.' What lies! *Pause.* What do you do? What do you do with a boy like that — let him go to jail? *Pause.* 'To be divided among my children *per stirpes* . . .' *Per stirpes.* Who gives a damn! *Pause: then he groans.*

GIRL:

    Are you okay?

OLD MAN:

    Have to sort those papers. Get at it tomorrow, first thing.

GIRL:

    How long will it take?

OLD MAN:

    I don't know. I'm the only one can do it, though.

GIRL:

    Before you die?

      Pause.

OLD MAN:

    I'll make time.

GIRL:

    How d'you know?

      Pause.

OLD MAN:

    I'll feel better tomorrow.

GIRL:

    Hmph.

      The faraway guitar begins to play again.

OLD MAN:

    So, I'd better be going. Sun's almost down.

GIRL:

    I can still see.

OLD MAN:

    Haven't you finished sorting those leaves?

GIRL:

    Nearly.

OLD MAN:

    You'd better come with me, let me see you on your way.   *Rises.*

GIRL:

    Sure. We'll go together.

OLD MAN:

    That fellow with the guitar's at it again.

GIRL:

    I know.

·OLD MAN:

    Sad. A lament. Why doesn't he play something lively? Here,
let me help you.

       He joins her, awkwardly, on the ground.

GIRL:

    You afraid to die?

OLD MAN:

    Me? Why do you . . .

GIRL:

    Just wondering.

OLD MAN:

    There, you see — wondering! You just wonder, keep on
wondering, and you'll be all right.

GIRL:

    Well, *are* you?

OLD MAN:

    Oh, no. Most of my friends are gone. Only I'd like it to be
unexpected. Don't want to dry up gradually, like some of them;
faculties going, one by one . . . limbs failing . . . eaten away
inside . . . knowing it's coming. Just turn the page one day and
find it there.

GIRL:

    What's it like, d'you think?

OLD MAN:

    Dying? *Jovially.* Well, an old fellow in a white
nightshirt comes along, toting a scythe over his shoulder. He

taps you with a bony finger and says here I am. It's time.

GIRL:

How d'you know?

OLD MAN:

Oh, I hear tell. But I'm going to give him a run for his money.

GIRL:

He might surprise you.

OLD MAN:

Oh, I hope he will! You only die when you join the past, become a memory like the rest of them, forget. Surprise! That's life! You remember that, now.

GIRL:

Sure.

    Pause.

OLD MAN:

You're a funny kid. Collecting dead leaves, a dead bird.   *Pause.*   But you've certainly cheered me up! Talking to you . . . Come on now — pick up your bag, let's get on our way.   *He rises with effort.*   Oh, I'm so stiff!

GIRL: *Rising.*

Are you feeling okay?

OLD MAN:

I — feel — wonderful! I never felt better in my life, if you want to know. Are you my friend?

GIRL:

Sure.

OLD MAN:

If I came back tomorrow, would you be here?

GIRL:

Maybe.

OLD MAN:

What would you like to do tomorrow? We could —

GIRL:

Climb trees?

OLD MAN:

That's what we'll do!

GIRL:

Like this one?

OLD MAN:

Just like that!

GIRL:

Show me!

OLD MAN:

It's getting dark!

The guitar becomes more rhythmical and excited.

GIRL:

That doesn't matter!

OLD MAN:

You want me to climb this tree?

GIRL:

Try! Try it now!

OLD MAN:

All right!   *He attempts to climb.*   I'll show you how it's done! When I was a boy . . . ! If I can just . . . ! Now . . . !   *He groans and falls to the ground.*

GIRL:

Ah! *She runs to him, and cradles his head.*

There is a long pause in the guitar music; then the mournful lay starts gently up again. It begins to move closer.

OLD MAN: *Painfully.*

I couldn't . . . I'm not . . .

GIRL: *Gently.*

You don't hate me, do you?

OLD MAN:

What? . . .

GIRL:

For coming now.

OLD MAN:

A little girl . . .

GIRL:

Who knows?

OLD MAN:

. . . with a brown-paper bag . . .

GIRL:

It was time, that's all.

The sound of the guitar moves much closer now. It is all around us. Then it dies away as the Old Man dies.

The little Girl rises and holds out her hand to him.

THE LIGHTS FADE.

Other dramatic works by Mavor Moore:

Published/Recorded:

Louis Riel (opera: music by Harry Somers); Centrediscs, Toronto (libretto and complete recording).
Inside Out (one-act); in *Three Canadian Plays*, Simon & Pierre, Toronto.
The Roncarelli Affair (TV play, with F.R. Scott); in *The Play's the Thing*, McMillan Canada.
Customs (one-act); *in Cues and Entrances,* Gage, Toronto; Earplay, USA (disc).
The Book of Hell (radio play): CBC Enterprises (tape)
Abracadabra (opera: music by Harry Freedman); Canadian Music Centre, Toronto.

Translations published:

Yesterday the Children Were Dancing (Gélinas); Clarke Irwin, Toronto.
The Puppet Caravan (Marie-Claire Blais); in *Joie de Vivre*, Copp Clark, Toronto.

Adaptations:

Sunshine Town (libretto & music), fr. Stephen Leacock's "Sunshine Sketches of a Little Town," 1953/1956
The Optimist (libretto & music), fr. Voltaire's "Candide." 1955
The Ottawa Man (comedy), fr. Gogol's "Inspector-General," 1961
Johnny Belinda (libretto: music by John Fenwick), fr. Elmer Harris' play. 1969
Fauntleroy (libretto: music by Johnny Burke), fr. Frances Hodgson Burnett's "Little Lord Fauntleroy." 1980
A Christmas Carol (libretto & music), fr. Charles Dickens' novel. 1988